# A Better World Starts Here:

## Activists and Their Work

I0414791

STACY RUSSO

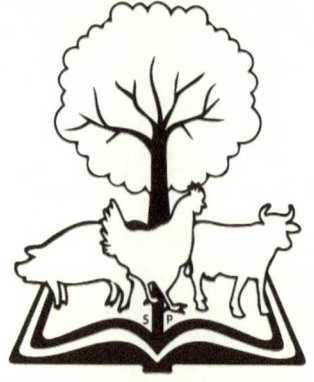

Sanctuary Publishers

**ISBN-13: 978-0-9989946-6-6**

Sanctuary Publishers, www.SanctuaryPublishers.com

-A Book Publisher That Gives Back-

Designer: Danae Silva Montiel
Content Editor: Julia Feliz, www.JuliaFeliz.com
Cover Art: Stacy Russo

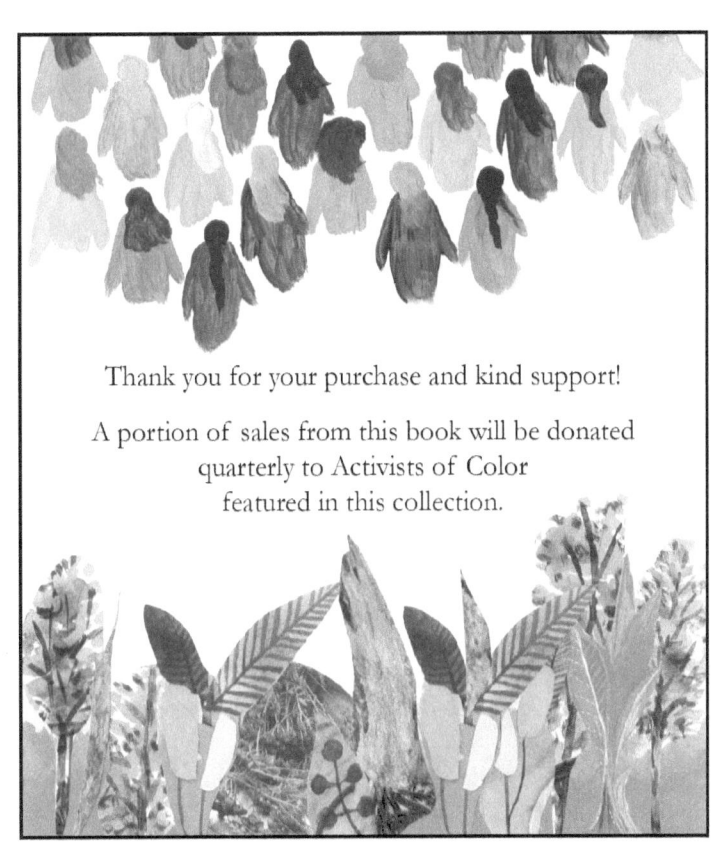

Thank you for your purchase and kind support!

A portion of sales from this book will be donated
quarterly to Activists of Color
featured in this collection.

for my brother, David

for the love and kindness

and enthusiasm for life

he freely shared

with everyone he met

(1961 – 2019)

*We have the power within us to create the world anew.*

– Grace Lee Boggs

# CONTENTS

*We are the ones we have been waiting for.*

– June Jordan

# 1 INTRODUCTION

In my work as a librarian, accessibility is a core ethical responsibility that involves combating discrimination and exclusionary practices and making sure library services and resources are available to everyone in the community. As a writer, I think of accessibility in a related way and especially with activist and social justice writing.

For activism to be most effective, I believe it needs to be accessible to the largest number of people possible. Many excellent works by activists come out of academia; unfortunately, the writing is scholarly and possibly only accessible to an audience well-versed in that specialized jargon. As an academic person myself, I acknowledge the importance of this work; still, I find highly theoretic writing and academic language sometimes difficult to sort through and engage with. I have also witnessed people I love, including my parents, struggling to understand, enjoy, or connect to such writing.

This led me to consider: Is it possible that there is an abundance of social justice writing in the world that is simply not accessible and, therefore, not reaching the people who would be inspired and empowered by it the most? How can we make activist writing more accessible?

One avenue for building connections and a strong activist community through writing is storytelling. Both the listening and the telling of a story can be forms of activism, because stories are often accessible and less theoretical and academic in tone, yet can help pass on knowledge, lessons, warnings, and so forth.

You are about to encounter people who are working toward a better world through first-person narratives gathered through one-on-one conversations in an effort to capture each activist's story. I'm hopeful that they will be accessible to you and any loved ones you wish to share this collection with. I also hope that you will be moved to take up the work needed at a time in which our world truly needs it.

### The Importance of Amplifying Activist Stories

Every activist has their unique, beautiful, and passionate story. My activism story began in the 1980s, when I was a teenager growing up in Southern California. Through the music and cultural movement surrounding the punk rock scene, I was awakened to do-it-yourself (DIY) ethics and social justice issues. It was a turning point in my life for which I will always be grateful. I became aware of the intersections of oppression related to human rights, animal rights, class inequalities, racism, women's rights, environmentalism, and so much more. Along with many of my friends at the time, I stopped eating meat. We went together to animal rights protests, anti-war marches, and demonstrations against nuclear proliferation. One of the most important realizations I made during these times was that there were many ways to create and live a life. I realized one could live a life as a political statement; that activism could truly be a way of life.

Imagine how much better the world would be if we held different values as a society. Imagine if we shifted our focus towards working against oppression and making the world more just. What if we invested more time on understanding social justice issues and learning from those working for a more just world? What if activism were given the time, exposure, and veneration we see celebrities and the wealthy being given without much thought or effort?

In an attempt to facilitate this exposure and understanding, this project turns the spotlight onto activists – those who dedicate their lives and work for liberation and the common good. In this book, you will find a diverse collection of personal stories that celebrate various forms of activism through interviews and narratives examining the early lives, political awakenings, and, ultimately, the paths that led activists around the world to the work they perform. You will find activist stories that include anti-racist action, feminist and women's rights work, art activism, animal rights work, LGBTQIA+ activism, environmental activism, food justice action, human rights work, and mindfulness education and practice within an activist context.

It was a goal from the beginning of the project to be

as inclusive as possible. Therefore, the activists included share very different life experiences, socioeconomic backgrounds, ages, education, race, ethnicity, gender, and other important aspects of their identities. Because of this, you will see people approaching their lives and their activism in various ways. Although it may not be possible for you to identify with every story found here, I hope that you will find stories that inspire and resonate with your life. I am also hopeful that some aspects of what you read will ring true and validate parts of your experience and that you will be open and willing to learn from those whose journeys are different to your own.

Are you already an activist, but perhaps are feeling despair, disillusionment, or fatigue? My wish is that these beautiful stories will reignite your fire and affirm the wonderful community you are part of. If your activist fire is already burning bright and resilient, may these stories make the luminous thing you are glow even brighter.

Are you at a turning point in your life, perhaps reaching your middle or later years, and interested in doing more and possibly becoming an activist? Are you a student who is still trying to figure out your path in life after high school or college? Hopefully you will read something here that gives you an opening to start your own activist life. No matter what, I wish for everyone to discover, as I have, that although there is pain and struggle here, there is also hope, love, and resilience.

*Consistent Anti-Oppression in Activism*

*A Better World Starts Here* is a project rooted in the awareness of interconnections. Important to the understanding of the stories you will find in this book, we can begin to understand the value of this awareness through *intersectionality*, a term first used within a feminist context by Kimberlé Crenshaw in her 1989 paper 'Demarginalizing the Intersection of Race and Sex: A Black Feminist Critique of Antidiscrimination Doctrine, Feminist Theory and Antiracist Politics." Crenshaw explained how a single element of a person's identity, such as gender or race, cannot provide a complete understanding of a person's life experiences. Specifically, she centered Black women in her discussion and presented the "multidimensionality" of Black women's experiences. Through this, Crenshaw demonstrated how a "single-axis framework," such as focusing only on race or gender, leads to a "marginalization of Black women in feminist theory and antiracist politics."

A way to understand Crenshaw's intersectionality is to imagine something that we are all familiar with– the intersection of a street. This resembles each of us and our complex identities. Although we are one complete being, similar to the meeting of different streets at the intersection, there are many components that make up who we are, including, but certainly not limited to, our gender, age, race, ethnicity, economic class, experiences of trauma and abuse, cognitive differences, and physical ableness. Some of these elements may give us privilege – even great privilege, such as being white in a systematically racist world. Regardless, it is important to be aware of these intersecting identities, which affect every individual to varying degrees depending on the number of intersecting identities each person has. In this way, we can become aware of and understand what it means to be privileged and also recognize when we may be in the role of the oppressor and when others are being systematically oppressed.

By adopting a lens that is aware of these interconnections, we are able to become more aware that there is no such thing as a single story. In working to recognize this and in implementing this awareness in our daily lives, we are then able to listen to, discover, and acknowledge multiple stories based on points of views and lenses different to our own. Through this, we begin to see and understand interconnections. We realize that movements toward liberation must be movements against all forms of oppression and hate.

An evolution in our understanding of this way of seeing the world and working towards *consistent anti-oppression* (a term coined by author Julia Feliz Brueck specifically within a vegan context in order to bridge gaps between social justice movements) is that we can ultimately extend our work and understanding beyond human beings to include all living beings and the natural world. This is why you will also discover vegan and environmental activists within this book. To be consistently anti-oppression in our activism and awareness allows us to understand that to combat all forms of oppression, our activism cannot be single-issue based, but must be intersectional at its core.

While talking with the beautiful individuals found herein, it became evident that, even if their activism has a particular focus, they have an understanding of the intersections of oppression and suffering. Michelle Carrera, founder of Chilis on Wheels, for example, shared how animal rights brought her to human rights. Her work, which includes providing vegan meals to the poor and homeless, is a testament to her desire for liberation for all beings. Sonya Renee Taylor, founder of The Body is Not an Apology, a movement committed to radical self-love, discusses the intersections of racism and ageism, as well as discrimination based on disability. Steve Bell, an advocate for prisoners through his work with the Prison Library Project, also provides support for victims of elder abuse through his additional volunteerism. Ardeth De Vries's work with Old Dog Haven involves finding a last refuge or home for senior dogs, but when I spoke with her, she discussed how the work is ultimately helpful for creating a better world for all aging beings.

All of these stories demonstrate how peace and justice work is not a straight line but should be envisioned much more as a web or intricate collage. Activism that understands these interconnections will set us *all* free.

Stacy Russo
Santa Ana, California
January 2019

*Cited Works*

Crenshaw, K. (1989). Demarginalizing the Intersection of Race and Sex: A Black Feminist Critique of Antidiscrimination Doctrine, Feminist Theory and Antiracist Politics. *University of Chicago Legal Forum*. Vol. 1989 (1), pages 139-167.

STACY RUSSO

*Tell me, what is it you plan to do with your*

*one wild and precious life?*

– Mary Oliver

STACY RUSSO

# 2 ACTIVIST INTERVIEWS

STACY RUSSO

## Aquila Hope

Trans Activist / Certified Holistic Life Coach

www.AquilaHope.com

—

"Through stories, we get the emotional core of an injustice. Stories move us to think of how we can find a solution."

*In 2017, Aquila Hope gave a talk on her personal journey for a Trans Day of Remembrance event. The talk became the pivotal moment in which she embraced her commitment to activism. That same year, Aquila co-founded the support group TranSpectrum as a safe gathering space for those who do not identify as cisgender. She has also recently started her practice as a Certified Holistic Life Coach. Herein, Aquila discusses her path to becoming an activist and the significance of the three pillars of her work: kindness, resilience, and creativity.*

—

I was born in the early 1980s in the middle of the United Kingdom, in Birmingham. I was raised in a place called Handsworth, which has a lot of history in terms of Black movements and social movements. The biggest would probably be the reggae music scene. A lot of bands came out of Handsworth, with Steel Pulse being one of the well-known ones.

Handsworth has a vibrant scene involving People of Color, including Black people and people from South

Asia or Far East Asia. The area is multicultural, and the larger surrounding area of Birmingham is very diverse. There are loads of cultures cross-pollinating and having conversations with one another.

My teenage years were great, but I was a sensitive kid. There was a period in my early-to-mid teens when I was angry at everything. I went to college at age sixteen and focused on math and other important areas, but I still found a lot of space for my creative life. I'm also a musician— a singer and a guitarist.

In many ways, I was a sheltered kid. I wasn't out partying all of the time. My world was geek culture. I was a video gamer, and I liked talking about animation with friends. This is still my culture, but obviously, it now spans out quite wider than that.

I got married ridiculously young, when I was about twenty. The marriage took up most of my twenties, but it did not work out. When I was twenty-eight, I went through a series of changes. I realized I wasn't straight, and I didn't fit my assigned gender. I went through a discovery of finding out where I stood and how I relate to my gender and sexuality as not just being trans but also non-binary. Not only did things change in the way I saw myself, but also how I saw things out in the world changed. I became an activist. Around this time, close to 2017, I also became homeless. I've had a lot of homelessness in my life, until very recently.

***Thank you for sharing that part of your life story. It sounds like your activism is a new part of your life***

*over the last few years. How did you become an activist?*

In 2017, I was invited to talk about my journey for a Trans Day of Remembrance event. Trans Day of Remembrance is an international annual event held to memorialize those who have been murdered as a result of transphobia. Even though I'm a performer, I wasn't used to making speeches. I was used to singing in front of people and reading poetry, but I was not used to just speaking. I was scared as heck, but I did it! That was the beginning of my actually starting to speak to people about injustices and the start of my embracing my role as an activist. I had been in environments in which social change was fostered, but this was when I pushed a button and started doing activism work. Before this, I dipped my toes a bit in local politics and also got involved some with the Labor Party; but I was jaded by politics in general and did not find it engaging. I have since realized that the political environments I had been exposed to were not about making actual, physical change. They weren't tactical about truly making change and moving forward.

My trans activism is at the top of what I do, but it cascades into all of these other areas, including healthcare, housing, and homelessness. I see the interconnections with these different things. What I see now is that trans individuals are being treated horribly, in the way that lesbians and gays were treated in the 1980s. One of the reasons for their horrible treatment back then was because of HIV. Now, we see a rerun of the exact same treatment. Trans individuals are told we're a danger to children, to people in public bathrooms, and even in sports. We are told that we're cheating in sports, even though there has-n't been a case of one person who is trans actually winning anything at a high level, such as an Olympic medal. It can get wearying because of the number of people constantly talking about us like we don't exist even— though we are here, and we do exist.

In 2017, my friend and I formed a group as two trans people. I'm trans-feminine, and he's trans-masculine. While looking around for resources to make socializing with other trans people accessible to us, we found there was a divide between identities within the community itself. We thought, "Why not just bring everyone together, put us all in the same room, and we can all share our experiences?" That was when we formed TranSpectrum. It's a social and support group for people who do not identify as cisgender, the gender/sex they are assigned medically at birth, and those who are questioning their gender. The group is still active now, under different leadership.

***Let's talk about what you call the three pillars of your work: kindness, resilience, and creativity. Why is kindness important to you, and how is this part of your activism?***

Kindness is literally the only reason I'm still here. In this context, I'm speaking about kindness for myself. I have experienced so much, including sexual abuse, homelessness, depression, anxiety, PTSD, and gender dysphoria issues. In the midst of this, I've had the ability to look within, pick myself up, and be kind to myself.

Some people think of kindness as something weak or insignificant, but it is what holds everything together. It is more than just being nice. It takes *strength*. When you are practicing kindness, you can make a positive step towards someone. Even if someone is arguing with you, you can find a space within yourself that provides protection from the verbal attacks, but also allows you to be kind. Ultimately, I want to leave a positive impression on someone. If I'm rude, they will remember that. If I'm kind, that is a better way to leave a person, because it plants seeds for future discussion and, possibly, future understanding.

### *Tell me about resilience.*

If we understand kindness as taking a positive step, resilience is having the courage to keep on getting up. There have been times, even on a daily basis, when I was in the depths of depression, and it was hard to get out of bed. It's important to understand that some days are not going to be great. You just need to open the door, get outside, and make your best steps forward. Some days are going to be absolutely awesome. Some days are going to be a total washout. You still get up and carry on, every day. It is important to have people who are able to provide you with support; but, even still, kindness and resilience are what have kept me alive.

If I wasn't resilient, I would not be talking with you now. Resilience is something that can scare people, because they see an inner strength taking hold. Even if you are beaten down, suddenly, you reappear. Maybe you are poking your head up and you are kind of crawling, and people will say, "How on Earth are you doing that?" A lot of people have said to me, "How are you not bitter? How are you not mean? How are you not a super cold individual for how the world has treated you and how things have worked out?" It's because I realized that every day is a blessing. Every day is an attempt at getting things right.

## *Please tell me about the third pillar: creativity.*

Creativity is the ability to make something out of nothing. It does not need to be restricted to art. For example, there is an activist in South Central Los Angeles who does guerilla gardening. That is creativity at work. He is taking what he has and making use of it. Creativity is all around us, and we can tap into it. I believe everyone has an innate creativity that we can get in touch with and use for the greater good.

## *How has your journey taken you to becoming a certified holistic life coach?*

I have always been the kind of person that people would seek out to talk with about their problems. The more I talked with people, I realized that I was not actually answering their questions, but empowering them to find *their* answers, as well as giving them time and space to process their questions. At first, I thought life coaching was a very highbrow and airy kind of thing. When I went to take the course, I realized that it was grounded and similar to what I was already doing for people. I just hadn't been paid for it.

I started studying and reading about the different techniques for a life coach. After receiving the certification, I reached out to people. Each person I've coached has different goals, even if they first come to me saying they do not have any goals. Once I start talking with them and pulling the treads, they discover their goals. I give them the space to communicate and explore. Being a life coach is a form of my creativity.

*I read on your website that storytelling is something you use when you are working to empower people. How are stories important to social justice work?*

Stories are important because they are the point where injustices meet the actual human condition. When we hear someone telling their story about an injustice that happened to them, their parents, or relatives, we connect to the humanity. Stories get to the heart of the matter. I was just reading Patrisse Cullors's book, *When They Call You a Terrorist: A Black Lives Matter Memoir.* This is an important story. It allows us to understand what happened in this person's life that led to the founding of a social justice movement.

Through stories, we get the emotional core of an injustice. Stories move us to think of how we can find a solution. A story gives us the root of the problem and we build and grow from that point. This is why I love storytelling and believe stories are powerful. They can impact people to get involved and work against injustice.

*How do you see your activism journey evolving in the future?*

Because I'm a minority within a minority within a minority— being Black, Queer, trans, trans-femme, non-binary, and a person who has a history of mental health issues— I know it may take years to reach a position through the mainstream media where I can help more people. I believe it will take time for my voice to get traction, but I understand activism is not an overnight thing. There is a long period of time where you work on yourself, understand more of what can be done, and figure out the spaces you need to get into to make change. I know it is going to be a lot of hard work. You can be in the dirt working while keeping your eyes up toward the clouds. It is important to always remember why you are doing the work.

Telling my story is a means for me to ultimately help trans people to obtain the services they deserve, including healthcare, housing, and job security. Trans people need to be seen as human beings like everybody else. It is important for young people to receive helpful information so they can make decisions about their lives when they reach the age of consent. This is what drives my activism.

***How do you stay positive with your activism when there is so much violence and other forms of injustice?***

People keep me afloat. If I'm struggling and having a bad day, I know if I need a little pick-me-up and I can reach out to someone. I can rant with a friend about someone's privilege or talk about how a person was being mean. Medication and therapy have also helped me maintain my positivity but having a support network is key.

## Marisela Gomez

Gentrification Activist / Public Health Scholar

www.MariselaBGomez.com

—

"Love in a collective space is a form of justice."

*When Marisela Gomez completed her professional training at Johns Hopkins Schools of Medicine and Public Health, she did not leave Baltimore; she remained and continued her activism work in the community that had become her home. Marisela's activism is focused on race relations and working to assure equity for Communities of Color. She is a mindfulness practitioner who lived for nearly three years in a Buddhist monastery setting, including one year at Thich Nhat Hanh's Plum Village in southern France. Marisela is the author of <u>Race, Class, Power, and Organizing in East Baltimore: Rebuilding Abandoned Communities in America</u> (Lexington Books). She received a B.Sc. and M.Sc. from the University of New Mexico in Albuquerque and a Ph.D., M.D., and M.P.H. from Johns Hopkins University. Here, she discusses her work, how listening is an activist practice, and the concept of "root shock" experienced by displaced communities.*

—

When something is not right, you can feel it in your body. You *know* something is wrong. When we are young, we may not be outwardly practicing what we call "activism" or "justice work," but we can *feel* injustice in our cells, our bodies, and in our daily lives.

21

I grew up in Belize. My grandparents raised me after my parents migrated to the United States when I was two. My parents left Belize because they wanted to make a better living for us. They worked in the U.S. for eleven years and brought my brothers and I over when I was thirteen.

While growing up in Belize, it was clear to me that there was something different about our family. The neighborhood we lived in was not rich, or even middle class. Overt racism surrounded us. The darker you were meant the poorer you were. The darker you were meant the less power you had. I saw patterns with regard to who got resources and who didn't. An anti-Black sentiment was always present in Belize. Later, I discovered this was also the case in the U.S. and, ultimately, in any country I visited.

There were gender dynamics, too. I saw this in the way I was treated, relative to my brothers; and in the way my grandma was treated, even though she ran the house. No one spoke about gay people or queer people; if they did, it was in a derogatory way. I was aware from a young age of what was acceptable and what was not– a pecking order of acceptability. I think that solidified my way of knowing, even though it wasn't until I came to the United States that I learned the language, the platform, and the framework to articulate my understanding of separation, power, and oppression.

In 2018, my aunt passed away. This brought me to reflect on her life and my own, because we were close when I was growing up. She was a Catholic nun, and I realize now that I was politicized from listening to her talk about poor people, especially in rural Belize. She told stories about nuns going out into the rainforest to try and help people living in shacks who didn't have water, food, or access to healthcare. She was distraught that there was no systematic support for people who were the most vulnerable and had the greatest need. She started to sow the seeds of what is just, equitable, and fair. Maybe this was not from within a systemic political analysis, but it was an understanding of right and wrong. This became part of what makes me an activist and a person who seeks justice from a place of love.

***Tell me more about your experience coming to the United States and what happened next in your life that led to activism work.***

I migrated to New Orleans, which is where my parents were living. That was a hard experience as a young Black-Brown mixed race —or creole, like we say in Belize — immigrant from a developing country. All the stories you hear about the way people are treated when they are new to the country are real— and exceptionally so in the current political atmosphere.

I was not encouraged in high school to go to college, even though I did fairly well. In Belize, I had excelled in school and even skipped a grade. However, I was pushed toward secretarial school in the U.S., and I ended up joining the Air Force when I was seventeen. I had no idea that college was a possibility for me. I was illusioned into thinking that joining the military would be a good thing, but it was no different from other experiences I had. The person on the lowest rung of the ladder is least valued and treated like they are inferior to those at the top. If you do not have any higher education, if you are not white, if you are queer or come from any marginalized group, if English is not your first language…They certainly let you know that you're not what they want.

Deciding to go to college was a political act. I believed higher education would be a way *out* of poverty and injustice and a way *in* to places in which I could influence change. I started taking university classes in the evenings, while I was in the military. I made a commitment to finish college by the time I finished the Air Force. It meant going to college full-time and being in the military full-time, but I did it. I was motivated because I was seeking justice for myself.

Later, when I was in Albuquerque, New Mexico, getting a master's degree, I became more aware of neighborhoods that were vacant and dilapidated. I started seeing the same pattern over and over again, with poor and darker-skinned people segregated from neighborhoods with access to resources. I moved to Baltimore, Maryland, to get a Ph.D. at Johns Hopkins. People like me don't usually get to go to schools like that. I had this clear intention in my mind of wanting to see if the people there put their clothes on the same way I do. I wanted to see if they ate the same way I eat. I had been socialized to believe that people in places like that are different from me – they're better and smarter than I am. That was my scientific experiment and, sure enough, we all know the result of that kind of experiment. I better understood the transactional nature of higher education and its sexist, racist, and classist actions.

By simply being present, I experienced and participated in the elitism of the "academy." It felt like taking a bath in dirty water.

### How did your activism grow while you were at Johns Hopkins?

I don't know how everyone doesn't become an activist when they go to the medical campus at Hopkins, because all you see is a white Ivy League institution that centers itself in the middle of this poor, Black community. It doesn't matter what window you are looking out from; all you see around you is poverty. That kind of clear demarcation, separation, and segregation, it moves you to act. I like to imagine that if everyone could see that, they would be moved to act.

What is obvious is the institutional oppression from a white institution in a Black community, the historical and current exploitation of poor Black people by the institution, and the historical and current exploitation of people for research. All of the ingredients were there to form a person who would become an activist. My focus in activism has been around race and class and how to remedy injustice and segregation, but this does not remove my awareness and interest in other forms of injustice, the interdependence of their origins and domination.

### Tell me more about your activism work in Baltimore.

I studied at Hopkins for fourteen years while, at the same time, organizing in the community surrounding the university. When I finished my professional training, I did not have the inclination to leave, like most of my colleagues. I was embedded and had formed a network there. I had community relationships in Baltimore that had been fostered by my work with other organizers, activists, and people in the neighborhood. There was a home for me, beyond the university. There was so much work to do.

To this day, I continue to feel an obligation to the community that surrounds Johns Hopkins. There is a dependency between any university or institution and the community around it. Anyone who has attended an institution has done so only through the grace of interaction between institution and community. When there is a disparity in power, exploitation of the community occurs. I'm not saying that institutions don't contribute to their communities, but it's important to consider how the nature of these contributions change depending on the race and class of the community. Johns Hopkins, for example, is the biggest employer in the city of Baltimore, yet who is working in all of the service positions and the kitchens? Black people are, including recent migrants. It's like redlining within employment.

In addition, why do nurses and other hospital staff need to unionize and protest to earn a living wage on which they can actually live in communities that are healthy? This is where we see how wage inequity leads to housing inequity and neighborhoods with differing life expectancies. We see how we continue to fabricate a society of separate and unequal. As gentrification continues around the institution, we see how the interaction between community and institution changes. We're happy to not segregate from certain people, but we are very happy to segregate from others.

***One of the concepts related to the disruption of***

*communities is "root shock," which you mention in one of your public talks. Can you explain this concept and how displacement impacts neighborhoods?*

The term "root shock" was introduced by Dr. Mindy Thompson Fullilove, a social psychiatrist from the New School in New York City. The term came out of her research in communities, such as Pittsburgh, that went through urban renewal. Large numbers of communities had been uprooted and displaced. *Root shock* is used to describe how people continuously become uprooted out of their communities, causing a shock to their systems. It's similar to when you pull a plant out and try to replant it. Different things can happen to that plant, depending on the status of the plant when you uprooted it, and the earth into which it is replanted. Even with the best intentions, sometimes the plant doesn't survive.

When we pull and displace people from their communities, something terrible happens to them and their systems go through shock, too. They may be relocated into a community that supports them, but they may not. It could be that the place they find is worse than the place from which they were uprooted. All of these things have an impact on how they survive.

Dr. Thompson Fullilove's work supports Marc Fried's studies on the negative health effect of forced displacement and relocation in a Boston neighborhood. The research showed that we need to take better care when we plan how we do community building in places like East Baltimore, where current urban renewal-like strategies continue serial forced displacement, because root shock is real and has generational impact on health and wealth.

*I would also like to know about how mindfulness became a part of your life and activism. I read that you spent time at Thich Nhat Hanh's Plum Village. Can you tell me about this experience?*

I stayed at Plum Village for a year and, once back in the U.S., I spent almost two years at one of the sister monasteries in upstate New York. Going to Plum Village changed my life. I had been working as a medical director for the Department of Juvenile Services. I was so disappointed with what I saw and how the system worked, I decided I didn't want to participate any more in that kind of work.

At this time, Johns Hopkins was starting a huge gentrification project to build a biotech park that would displace more than 750 nearby households. I started working as the organizer, and then the director, of a group that formed (SMEAC) to challenge the way Hopkins was handling the project. It was a violent and pathological struggle. When people with money want land, they'll behave in oppressive ways, especially if they think the people who have the land aren't worthwhile. I became burnt out as an activist and organizer. I can't imagine what it was like for the residents who were born and raised in East Baltimore. Some people had been there generationally, living out yet another displacement for development.

About ten years before this, I started reading about Buddhism and meditating. As I started meditating, I began getting into contact with all of this anger. I saw how a lot of the justice work I did was fueled by anger and rage. It wasn't just the anger of that particular injustice or struggle I was involved in; it was *collective* anger built up from many years– generational and ancestral anger. I realized I couldn't keep running off of that anger.

After starting my meditation practice, folks around me were noticing that I wasn't as angry and asking me why. I saw how effective I could be if I wasn't as angry, so I decided it was time to leave spaces that ran on anger.

It's unfortunate that we are fueled and trained in many justice struggles to have the angriest person in the lead, and to cultivate anger in others. I became more conflicted around this, so I decided to leave for a year— which turned into three! I also took another year to wander on a solitary retreat. During my wandering journey, I lived in places near the water, by myself. I lived in Belize for six months. Two of those months were spent in a tent in the jungle. I lived on Smith Island, an island in Maryland that you can only reach by a forty-minute ferry ride, for seven months.

Nurtured by the stillness of body and mind, I was able to look internally. I had made a commitment to not speak. I told myself to shut up and not just listen to people but to listen to what was going on inside of me. Following this time of my life, I was invited to return to Baltimore and write the history of what happened during the organizing work of the biotech park. I saw this as opportunity to come back and tie up loose ends, as well as decide what I would do next. This was about eight years ago.

**Tell me more about the importance of listening. How did listening became a part of your activism?**

What I learned is that listening is not just an external practice. Listening is also internal. Can I be still enough to listen to what's inside myself at any moment? It's important to be able to listen beyond the immediate emotion that rises up in us at the spur of the moment. If people are saying mean, racist, or sexist things, it's easy to react. This is because it stings us. We all have history that must be healed. If we have the space to listen to what is happening inside of us at that moment, it's going to shift how we respond, because our response will be coming from a different place. The response will come from a clarity that knows anger or hatred is there. A mind aware and observing of anger is different from a mind submerged in anger; it's a different energy. We can't be violent, oppressive, or unjust in our work of justice. It's contradictory to our efforts.

There are some questions to consider. When we are listening outside, can we listen from a place of compassion? Can we listen from a heart space? In this space, one attempts not to minimize a person or situation into binary or dualistic occurrence. A heart space invites in the grey, the pieces that are not apparent; and it realizes our shared humanity. Before responding, we can then ask ourselves if we are able to hold the person as a whole in our mind. The concept of holding an entire person flows from the heart space.

An example of how I would apply this would be in dealing with a greedy developer displacing Black people. They are not just a greedy developer; they are also a parent, someone who gets a common cold, and is loved by someone just like me. It doesn't mean I do not hold them accountable. It means my action comes from a space of assessing the violence or potential violence *and* also acknowledging their humanity. This allows my responses to come from a place of compassion. However, this compassion does not always look "kind." Sometimes compassion is sharp, and to someone who does not fully understand what is happening, it may feel harsh, wrongheaded, or incongruous with love.

If I can remember in a charged moment of injustice and pain, in which the perpetrator is acting from ignorance, greed, or jealousy, that, at times, I act from those places, too, then I have connected to our shared humanity *–and* I can still act to stop this negative thing from happening. If I only see this person as greedy or ignorant, without seeing *all* of them, I am acting from a place of thinking I am above them. Here, I have gone to a dualistic way of thinking, in which someone is either good or bad. At this point, I have disconnected myself from this human being. This is not a very insightful place to be, but it is often the way we behave. An awareness helps us to see all of this; for me, that's part of my activism. It's a different way of coming into spaces and working for justice.

**Where has your activist journey taken you to at this moment in your life?**

Right now, I'm part of groups that are trying to build alternative communities and movements, such as collective residential communities of people who seek justice seeded in love. This includes building alternative communities that want to figure out how to create new ways for wealth building in abandoned Black and Brown communities. It's different from fighting a development project that's trying to move people out of their homes. Instead, we are asking, "How are we going to build something alternatively that can remedy this injustice that's here?"

I want to focus more on rebuilding things with love at the core. It's important when we think of change to imagine how we can bring something more beautiful into a space. How do we bring something more equitable? How do we bring something more just? We can create something that is so beautiful and good and powerful that it will take care of the bad thing that is out there. Love in a collective space is a form of justice.

### How do you continue to stay positive in your activism?

This is an important question. Perhaps the most important. I say this because I find myself constantly remembering to do just this. Often, I forget. I forget the beauty and wonder of this life. I try to remember that there is much to be grateful for: the rose bush still holding space for a moment of pause on this cold wintery morning in Baltimore. I stopped and gave it gratitude with a smile and a sniff. Wonderful. The dance of yellow, orange, and red leaves in the light, there for me when I notice. And the breath, always there when I remember to return to it. It's easy to get drawn down into the injustices: another subsidized gentrification project; illegal arrest of another young Black man, for 'standing while Black'; cut back of programs for the mentally ill in states like Louisiana. So, this practice of mindfulness is not an option in our work of justice. It's necessary. Because we must continuously remember to come back to the present moment and recognize the preciousness of all that is available for us and not only the challenges.

How do I remember? Daily meditation or contemplation practice is key for me. Daily yoga or some type of stretching movement; walking or running at least 5 days of the week; listening daily to talks about generosity, healing, understanding, cultivating a more aware mind; sharing laughter or a healthy meal/a cup of tea with a friendly personality; being in nature; getting sufficient rest when possible; smiling for no reason (it relaxes the muscles of the face and is contagious!). It can be an entirely suffering world we experience every day when we forget to remember the many blessings. I take time to have a day of mindfulness each week, turn off the devices, notice my steps, wash the dishes like there is nothing else to do but just that... and immediately space is created in my mind, heart, body, and spirit. I must remember to gladden the mind and the heart each day, to constantly invite sacred into my steps, each moment. This remembering, this awareness, determines where and how I bring the mind to be in this world. These types of practices nourish a happiness that does not harm, prevent burn out, and keeps me fresh and clear that this journey of justice must move with integrity and love.

STACY RUSSO

**Sandi Torkildson**

A Room of One's Own

www.RoomOfOnesOwn.com

—

"Books are powerful."

*In 1975, Sandi Torkildson and several of her women college friends founded A Room of One's Own, a feminist bookstore in Madison, Wisconsin. The store would become much more than a bookstore; it was, and continues to be, a vibrant community space. Herein, Sandi reveals how new ideas discovered in women's studies classes in the early 1970s led a group of young women to raise enough money to start a feminist business that became a source of hope, support, and inspiration for a community. She also discusses the solidarity between feminist bookstores throughout the country before large chain bookstores and online booksellers resulted in the closure of most of the stores. At the time of this writing, A Room of One's Own is celebrating its forty-third anniversary.*

—

I come from a very large family– I have ten brothers and sisters. Most of my early life was spent outside of Milwaukee, on a small farm. My dad still worked in the city, at a brewery; but he moved us to the country because it was more affordable. I think he also thought we would have a better life in the country, since he had grown up on a farm. Our own family farm was not a commercial farm. We mostly raised food for ourselves and had a little farm stand stocked with what we grew from our large garden. What I can say about my early life is that it taught me how to work hard!

By the time I was in high school, a lot of people were leaving Milwaukee, and the suburbs were being developed. My parents sold the farm for a good price around 1964 and ended up buying a house and moving back into the city. This exposed me to a different world. Before the move, I had mostly only interacted with white Norwegian farmers. When we moved to Milwaukee, I attended a high school that had African-American students and other students of color. This helped expose me to different cultures. Having only known farm life up to that point, I felt somewhat like an outsider. These feelings changed once I started exploring the city.

Among the things I discovered in my new home were bookstores; I had never been to one before. I remember Schwartz's Bookstore in downtown Milwaukee. That was in the mid-1960s, when all of the avant-garde poets and small presses were publishing. This was a whole different world to me. The Civil Rights movement was also happening in Milwaukee, and I remember seeing protest marches go right past our house.

At this time, they were ripping down a big part of the inner city to build an expressway, which ended up never being built— even though they tore down whole neighborhoods just to make room for it. Some kids I went to school with were being affected by this, and I became more aware of social issues and different types of inequality and poverty that I had not been aware of while living out on a farm.

## *After high school, did you go to college?*

Yes. I enrolled in engineering school, since I was very good at math. My brother was studying engineering and had convinced me to pursue it as well. My dad had worked as a mechanical engineer for the breweries, but he did not finish college. Back then, you could become an engineer by experience and passing a test. In my family, college was looked upon as where you went to get a job.

I was a strong woman, but I didn't feel that I fit in with engineering. I was one of a few women in any of the classes that I took. The other women were really brilliant. Even though I was good at math, I felt I wasn't as smart in engineering as they were. It was a struggle for me. I worked hard, but I didn't feel welcome; I felt like an outsider, again. My professors did not like that I had a hard time in their classes. They also didn't like that I spoke up against their off-color jokes, so they would comment about it saying things like, "Oh, I guess I can't tell that joke 'cause Sandi's in the room." It started to raise my consciousness about women and how we were restricted in these spaces. I don't think I could articulate the experience at that time, but it certainly felt that I was not welcome in certain areas.

I had a great English teacher. She was a single woman who was really instrumental in introducing me to literature, especially literature with strong female characters. I wouldn't say that I was conscious of being a feminist, but the feminist movement was starting then, so I was aware of it. I ended up changing my major to U.S. American studies. With this major, I was able to take English, history, and sociology classes.

## *What ultimately happened that led to the creation of the feminist bookstore?*

There was a lot of social-justice-related activity happening while I was in college. I fell in with a group of women who were taking classes at the university extension. Back then, there weren't many professors that were women. Many of the women who had been awarded their Ph.Ds. were relegated to being professors in university extension classes. These professors began teaching Women's Studies 101 in the evenings. If you were a student at the university, you could take the extension classes for free or for a minimal fee. I found these classes to be eye-opening; through them, I developed the group of friends that ultimately led to the bookstore.

We would go to class in the evening and come out excited and wanting to talk about these new ideas. We did not feel we had a place to go to do so. There were no coffee shops, and we didn't feel bars were a place that we could go and discuss things without being bothered by men assuming that we wanted to hook up with them.

In these classes, we heard about a feminist bookstore in Chicago and another one in Minneapolis. I had worked part-time at a college bookstore, so I had some limited experience. We started to think, "Wouldn't it be great to have a space for women where we could go and talk about things?" We thought maybe a bookstore was the way to go.

We visited the feminist bookstores in Minneapolis and Chicago, and we began raising money to open our own. Everything started to come together. This was also the same time that a lot of small presses were forming, because printing became more accessible to people through cheap offset machines. Things that were not being printed by the mainstream presses were now appearing. We held fundraisers and raised $5,000 to open the store in an old office that had been a printing company in downtown Madison. In 1975, we officially opened A Room of One's Own.

### *How did it feel to see this dream realized?*

We were young, and felt we had nothing to lose. We didn't have families. We were just finishing school, so it was something on which we could take a chance. I think this all happened in my last year as an undergraduate. I ended up getting a degree in teaching and was working as a student teacher at the time. I would work at the bookstore after teaching. All the other women were finishing their degrees, too. They worked at the store for a while, but ultimately, they all went on to other things. I decided to stay because I enjoyed the work.

### *It sounds like you and the other women definitely saw the bookstore as a gathering space from the beginning. How was the store part of the community?*

The space was only 1,200 square feet. We had bookcases around the walls, but the whole center was a gathering space. We had a bright orange shag rug in the center with some chairs and an old table. We also originally partnered with a group called Wisconsin Women in the Arts, and they held art shows in the space. We had the typical book groups and readings, but we also had a lot of political and social action groups that would meet there for organizational purposes.

This was, of course, before computers, so people found roommates or discovered events through posters and bulletin boards. The whole entranceway for the bookstore was filled up with hundreds of posters. This was also at same time when shelters for battered women were opening, so there were advertisements for these, as well as resources on rape crisis support. In addition, we had information for women who wanted to learn certain trades, including ads from a couple of nuns that advertised auto mechanics courses especially for women so they would not be victimized and taken advantage of. We became a conduit for all of this information to be disseminated.

My sister came near Madison to go to law school, maybe three or four years after we started the store. She told us a story about an older woman in her class who spoke to them about having been battered. The woman had visited our bookstore and saw a poster about domestic abuse that we had placed in the shop. She said seeing that was the first time she realized what was happening to her and that it was not okay, so she called the crisis line on the poster, which led her down a path towards enrolling in law school in her forties. I have always cherished her story.

*It's powerful knowing your community-based bookstore could change lives. Once you started the bookstore did you remain in contact with other women's bookstores?*

Oh, yes! It was a movement! Carol Seajay out of San Francisco created a magazine called *Feminist Bookstore News*. I wrote articles and book reviews for the magazine. We would also get together in person. There were a number of women involved in national and global print conferences, in which publishers, writers, journalists, feminist bookstore owners, and others would gather. The feminist bookstore owners would come together for long weekends and hold workshops on everything from how to do finances to how to be more inclusive. We also held Feminist Bookstore Days, which were smaller events that were held before the U.S. American Booksellers Convention in different cities each year. We would have workshops at these events, too. It was a very exciting time. I really don't know how we pulled it all off!

***When did you start to notice that things were changing that ultimately led to so many of the bookstores closing?***

Feminist bookstores closed, along with a lot of independent bookstores, due to the growth of the chain stores. It wasn't really that long ago– possibly around fifteen years ago. It was getting hard for all of the smaller stores to compete with giants like Borders and Barnes and Noble. They seemed to have an endless amount of money and were opening up so many stores that they would saturate an area. The large stores were also understandably enticing, because it was wonderful to go in and see so many books for sale. Shortly after the growth of the chain stores, Amazon opened.

A lot of feminist presses and magazines also started to consolidate. More trade publishers were publishing content that only the feminist and smaller presses used to publish, which made it easier for more general bookstores to carry the books. One thing I've noticed is there's something still very different about the selection of books you see at an independent bookstore versus a store like Barnes and Noble.

It's important to consider not only what is ordered, however, but also how books are displayed and categorized. In our women's studies section, for example, we have a subsection on violence against women. In a bigger bookstore, these books may be put in a section related to criminology or sociology. Another example is the importance of having titles on display for which people may be too intimidated to ask. When incest became a major topic, we had the book *The Courage to Heal* on display to make it more accessible.

How things are displayed also makes people feel welcome— or not. Putting children's books that have People of Color on the cover is important all year round, not just during certain holidays or events like Black History Month. All members of the community need to see themselves reflected through the books on display.

***A Room of One's Own has managed to weather the storms of changing times. What is going on with the store now?***

I'm getting ready to retire soon, so I just sold the store a few weeks ago. The store is doing well. We have survived our competition. About six years ago, we moved to a much bigger space and merged with a used bookstore, so we became a more general independent bookstore. We have everything we had before but added more. We kept all of the same sections we had at the smaller store, so people can still easily find what they need.

Some people may just think of a bookstore as a business, but bookstores are different. They are centers for social change. That is why I did it for all of these years. Independent bookstores are important to communities because they give people a voice. When people are curious about something, they can go there and find information. Books are powerful. Literature exposes people to other people's lives. It is a form of education.

**How do you believe your work with *A Room of One's Own* contributed in the past to making the world better for marginalized people, and how do you see this continuing?**

Since the beginning, people could find books, periodicals, and even music that validated their lives at A Room of One's Own. This included married women, women coming out as lesbian, a young person unsure of their sexuality, or someone dealing with their family's response to their sexuality. We offered free space to others, such as a welfare rights group looking for a place to meet or a group of women artists looking for a place in which they could show their works when other places did not take their work as serious "art." Just to have a place you could come as a feminist to meet and talk to others that shared that view was important.

Like most feminist bookstores, though, we put other issues beyond gender in focus. We put books about racial and economic disparities and oppressions both inside the store and in window displays. We had, and continue to have, sections on Black studies, Latinx studies, disability rights, Native American studies, and many others. We train our staff to always suggest books that are not just about white people when recommending children's titles, and we make sure they use a diverse group of books for displays in the children's room. We have a large selection of Spanish-English bilingual books for both children and adults.

Beyond this, we encourage our staff to read from a wide range of authors and write up short reviews to encourage others to also read these titles. Supporting LGBTQIA+ rights has also always been important to us. We have helped to fund responses to hate groups that have put up anti-LGBTQIA+ billboards or protested against this community. We support the LGBTQIA+ books for prisoners and the local jail library project by raising money and supplying books to them. We also raise money to help low-income families get books to read to their children, and we support many groups by donating items and gift cards to their fundraisers. A feminist bookstore like A Room of One's Own is a community space.

## Carol J. Adams

Writer

www.CarolJAdams.com

—

"With activism work, all we have to do is start."

*Carol J. Adams is the author of the groundbreaking work <u>The Sexual Politics of Meat: A Feminist-Vegetarian Critical Theory</u>, which focuses on the linked oppression of women and non-human animals. She holds a Master of Divinity from Yale Divinity School. Carol has been a leading figure in the ecofeminist and animal rights movements, yet her activism extends beyond these areas and has always been focused on intersectional justice, including work related to domestic violence, fair housing, and anti-racist action. Her numerous book publications include <u>The Inner Art of Vegetarianism: Spiritual Practices for Body and Soul</u> (Lantern Books), <u>The Pornography of Meat</u> (Lantern Books), <u>Living among Meat Eaters: The Vegetarians' Survival Handbook</u> (Lantern Books), and <u>Protest Kitchen: Fight Injustice, Save the Planet, and Fuel Your Resistance One Meal at a Time</u> (Conari Press) with co-author Virginia Messina. A collection of her writings also appears in the <u>Carol J. Adams Reader: Writings and Conversations 1995-2005</u> (Bloomsbury Academic). Here, Carol discusses her early experiences with activism, different aspects of her social justice work, the importance of her veganism, and the practice of keeping a daily journal.*

—

I grew up in a small town in Upstate New York. A key to understanding my activism and my intellectual interest is that I had parents who were definitely equals. My father was a lawyer. My mother was a social activist, despite having grown up in a very conservative household. She told me a story about her mother, my grandmother, being sexually harassed by the farmer she worked for around 1912. She was chased around the kitchen table by him. I think this made my grandmother view the world as a very unsafe place for women. Because of this, my mother and her sister grew up living a very restricted life.

I understand my grandmother's anxiety. That's how she had experienced it in the early twentieth century, and the dangers she encountered persist in the twenty-first century. My mother decided she was not going to do that to her children, though; she became very liberal, and raised us liberally.

In the 1960s, my mother got involved in the movement to bring birth control to our county. She helped found a committee focused on these efforts, whose title I love: The Committee to Bring Family Planning Services to Chautauqua County. She was very indignant about the status of women. When my sister went to Vassar and was supposed to read *The Feminine Mystique*, my mother read it, too. She followed everything about the women's movement and was fascinated by the 1970 women's strike for equality.

She also learned about the plight of migrant workers. There were two kinds of migrant workers in Upstate New York at that time. One of the groups was made up of contract migrant workers from Puerto Rico. Farmers would fly down to a village and contract with the males of the family to come up in March or April or May or June.

My mother got involved in advocating for safe housing for them, going to the health department and confronting the farmers. She was sort of fearless.

My father, as a lawyer, represented people in a village near Lake Erie, which was being polluted. He had one of the earliest lawsuits on behalf of the environmental degradation of Lake Erie in the mid-60s. He also challenged the makeup of the jury pool for not having African-Americans on its list.

We flourished in a very intellectually-stimulating and activist house, in which activism was clearly just part of your lifeblood. It wasn't something you thought about; if there was injustice, you did something about it. It is a remarkable thing.

***That's wonderful. I can definitely see where the roots of your activism come from. When did veganism and animal rights become an aspect of your life?***

My father had this little law office building in our small town. Right behind it was a barn that a man named Butch had. He would sell cows and horses. He was also the local butcher. When we were growing up, he let us ride the ponies and horses. We'd come down and clean them and pet them. He also let us watch him butcher. I still remember watching a cow fall when he shot them. It was shocking; but, you know, children can be very bloodthirsty themselves. There was a real disconnect. I talk about the concept of an "absent referent" later in my writing. This is where the animal disappears conceptually as a being of their own value. The first step toward making them into meat is that the animal disappears as a living being,

through violence; and conceptually, as a being worth con-
sideration. Certainly, I was experiencing the animal become the absent referent, and animals were already absent
referents in my life. While I cared about the horses and
dogs, I was not in any way troubled to go home and eat
meat.

Then, in 1962, one of my father's clients saw three
cute girls running past my father's office. He asked who
they were, and, when he learned it was his attorney's children, and of our love for horses, he gave us the one we
loved most: Jimmy. Years later, in 1973, after my first year
at Yale Divinity School, I came home and was unpacking
when there was a knock at the door. A neighbor stood
there, exclaiming, "Someone's just shot your pony!" I ran
up to the pasture where the ponies were kept. The one
remaining pony was pacing back and forth and whinnying
and very upset; and there was Jimmy, lying dead on the
ground.

It was very shocking. We could hear gunshots in the
woods that bordered the pasture. Later, we found the
teenagers who'd been target practicing, but they swore
they had not shot Jimmy. You couldn't even tell whether
he had been killed by them or by a heart attack. (He was
an old pony.) That night at dinner, I was very upset. My
father said, "Let's just have hamburgers." I went up to the
only food store in town, next to my father's office, and
got some hamburger meat; but when I went to bite into
the hamburger, I thought, "This is meat from a dead cow.
I wouldn't eat Jimmy. Jimmy's dead up on the pasture,
and we're going to bury him tomorrow. So why am I eating a dead cow? Is it that I'll only eat animals I don't

know? Doesn't that make me a hypocrite?" I'd say that's what began the movement in my life toward veganism.

I was already involved in the feminist practice of consciousness-raising. A key part of consciousness-raising is asking questions about your own life and seeing how the political is personal and the personal is political. In a sense, I enacted that thought process by considering my own practice of eating animals. I became a vegetarian and, ultimately, vegan. Within about two weeks of becoming a vegetarian, I realized there was a connection between feminism and vegetarianism and began working on what would ultimately become my book, *The Sexual Politics of Meat.*

**I've noticed your activism is focused on the intersections of various forms of oppression. Has this always been the case or has that developed more over time for you?**

I think it's always been the case. I think there's been a misunderstanding of the second wave of feminism. The second wave is rightly critiqued for often presenting a white perspective or a middle-class perspective. Yet, it often postulated a feminism that recognized interconnections. I experienced the second wave as a part of feminist communities in New Haven, Boston, and Philadelphia. While at Yale Divinity School, I did fieldwork at an abortion clinic that was run by Yale New Haven Hospital, and I also worked at the New Haven Women's Liberation Center. The next year, I was a feminist intern for the Christian Association at the University of Pennsylvania. Especially notable at the Christian Association was our work against rape. This was in 1973 and 1974. I saw that feminism was constantly revising itself as it was being critiqued.

Right around that time is when the Black feminists organized the Combahee River Collective, which started issuing wonderful, incisive papers. Barbara Smith, Beverly Smith, and Demita Frazier took the name of their collective from a raid by Harriet Tubman that freed 750 enslaved people at the Combahee River in South Carolina in 1853. I remember the excitement many of us felt as we read their original statement ("The Combahee River Collective Statement") when it came out in 1977 and 1978. Their statement refers to "major systems of oppression as interlocking." They were also, apparently, the first to use the term "identity politics." (You can read about this in *How We Get Free: Black Feminism and the Combahee River Collective,* edited by Keeanga-Yamahtta Taylor.)

I feel that feminism has always had a part of itself that was aware of intersections. My feminist-vegan theory evolved out of my feminist perspective, and the feminist community in which I lived—the Boston-Cambridge community, where the women who started the Combahee River Collective also lived. I believe feminism is about the radical transformation of life for everybody on this planet. In the 80s, for example, my partner and I set up a hotline for battered women in this rural area of Upstate New York. I also got very involved in fighting for integrated housing. That was about a nine-year battle. Throughout the 1980s, as I was writing *The Sexual Politics of Meat,* my main job was as a community organizer and activist working to help poor people.

I write about the kind of anti-racist work I was doing then in an article titled "What Came before the Sexual Politics of Meat" [it's included in *The Carol J. Adams Reader* (Bloomsbury Academic)]. It became very obvious to me how racism draws on animalizing African-Americans, especially African-American men. My first article on this and the politics of solidarity was published in 1993 in *Neither Man nor Beast*, which just recently was released in a Bloomsbury Revelations edition.

***I'd like to know how you approach a situation in which you encounter people who are very passionate and possibly doing great work focused on human rights or environmentalism, but you discover they eat animals and they don't see the connection.***

I've been doing this work for forty years, so how I approach it has changed. For example, in the 1980s, when I was very involved at the state level in domestic violence work, I approached it a certain way. I remember going out with everybody that was on the Governor's Commission against Domestic Violence and on the State Commission on Domestic Violence and they would order hamburgers. I'd say to them, "But, how can you do that? This is a form of violence. We're against violence." I remember these conversations were particularly difficult.

I think people have knee-jerk reactions. They think that there is a limited amount of compassion and we're going to use it up on animals, so oppression against humans is not going to change. Or that in caring about animals, we are somehow allowing human oppression to continue. The only people who think you can't care about animal oppression and human oppression are those who continue to benefit from animal oppression. Meanwhile, we vegans, and especially we vegan feminists, are involved in working for reproductive freedom for *all*, *and* against domestic violence, *and* volunteering at homeless shelters, *and* doing many other activisms. Virginia Messina and I cover this issue in *Protest Kitchen,* when we answer the question, "Why do we care about animals when there are so many problems for humans?"

To begin with, asking that question may be failing to even understand the people for whom you're advocating. Sometimes homeless individuals are homeless because they love their animal companion and can't take that animal into the shelter. Sometimes battered women don't leave because the animal would be at more risk if they leave. Now, of course, we know that the people most affected by climate change are going to be poor people, especially People of Color in the Global South; and it is well-documented that meat-eating and dairy contribute to climate change.

To continue to think that the status of non-human animals is not related to social justice is clearly to not even understand the social justice problems of *humans* at this point. We need to help people understand that we can care about all of these issues simultaneously, and that some people are just better equipped to advocate for or care for animals. Those people should be allowed to express their skills in that way. It is not an either/or situation.

*I'd like to go in a different direction now and ask you about your practice of keeping a daily journal. I understand you have been doing this for over twenty years, and it has been an important practice for you. How does this relate to your activism work?*

Starting back in the 1970s, I kept something off and on. I even quote from a journal in *The Sexual Politics of Meat* at the beginning of Chapter Eight to show the kind of questions I was asking myself way back in 1976. In 1996, I read Julia Cameron's *The Artist's Way*, and this led to my keeping a daily journal. In the book, she suggested writing "morning pages," which I started doing. I later found out that this recommendation actually comes from a woman named Dorothea Brande, writing during the Depression in her book, *Becoming a Writer*.

The idea is that you write when you first wake up in the morning. Now I know a lot of people do not handwrite any more, and that people are *very* busy in the morning; but this is often when the subconscious is closest to us, including remembering our dreams. In 1996, within a month of starting to keep my journal, I also read *Adventure Inward* by Morton Kelsey, about the spiritual aspect of keeping a journal. This was very formative to my practice. He wrote, "It is important to remember that journal-keeping is a living process, like exercise. One does the same thing over and over to develop and maintain a skill. Healthy living in body and soul and mind requires the constant repetition of certain practices." I get up in the morning and write three pages or more in a dedicated journal.

Kelsey suggested that when you're keeping a journal, you should write your experiences, thoughts, and reflections from the front to the back; but, if you have an idea, go to the back and write from the back to the front so that later, you can easily find those ideas. For instance, if I'm writing along, and I suddenly have an idea, I will turn to the back of the journal and write. In looking back at journals from 2001 and 2002, I found that many ideas that appear in my book *The Pornography of Meat* are there, at the back of journals.

For ten years, I was a long-distance caregiver for my mother, who had Alzheimer's; and, at the same time, a caregiver for my mother-in-law, who lived with us and had her leg amputated. It was a very difficult, emotional time; but, in the midst of that, I started writing in my journal five things I was thankful for at the end of every day. It might've been, and still might be, as simple as food I made or a movie I watched or some kindness somebody did. It doesn't have to be earth-shattering things. It's just to remind me about the role of gratitude in all of our lives.

I also go back and try to reread my journals. I can go back to the journals from the time when I was caring for my mom, and there she is. If I miss her, I can go to my journal and find the sort of repartee that I had recorded just because I was recalling the day. I believe Kelsey said that a journal isn't complete until you re-encounter it.

I only write on one side of my journals. When I go back, I write the date at which I'm rereading it. And then I'll put comments on the other side of the page, so that the journal becomes something with which I'm interact-ing. I find a lot of serendipity related to which journal I decide to read at what time and how that intersects with what I'm experiencing as I read it. I think keeping a jour-nal is one of the greatest gifts I've given myself.

*I believe the practice may be helpful to others, so thank you for sharing. You mentioned caregiving. Did caring for elderly people impact you as an activist?*

It certainly reminded me of how caregiving is undervalued in our culture. One of the reasons is that it's done mainly by women in the family or by Women of Color as hired caregivers. I read a *New Yorker* article about women from the Philippines who come to the U.S. and work as caregivers. They send money back to their families, but they never see their own kids. Caregiving is a very privatized thing. They talk about how it takes a village to raise a child. I believe it takes a village to care for an elderly person.

I've written about this in a couple of places. I wrote a long essay for *Critical Inquiry* titled "Towards a Philosophy of Care through Caregiving." At the end of the article, I say that my veganism became more radical and deeper during my caregiving. I was very thankful for my veganism. It was something that nurtured me every day. It was something that gave back to me. There are many different ways that you can lose yourself in caregiving, and it is very exhausting. However, no matter what I was doing, there was my veganism every day to nourish me and remind me of some of my core commitments. I had a friend who always brought me vegan food, and my sisters made sure that there was vegan food in the house when I was the one coming in to care for my mom. My veganism felt like a gift to me.

Once you've been vegan long enough, it's just something you do, but suddenly it explodes in this new way, because you built the foundation. The foundation you were building, that you may have not been aware of, helps to nourish you during stressful times. It was always there to affirm who I was.

**Overall, when you think of your work, how do you see it contributing to make the world better for marginalized people?**

I want to be really careful about this, because I don't want to pretend that I know all of the answers or that there's some Lady Bountiful interaction going on or self-satisfied thought. I think the most important thing I'd say is we can never be satisfied with what we've accomplished because it implies that there was a goal and we've met it. I'm more interested in activism as a process.

There is a wonderful quote from Václav Havel, a poet and political dissident, who served as the last president of Czechoslovakia. This is a paraphrase of what he said, which is, "We work for change because we believe that's what's necessary. If the change comes, that's good. But even if it doesn't come, this is what we needed to do to be involved in social justice today." We cannot measure our successes in a linear way, because that sets us up for failures. We can't have the goal of success. We have to have the goal that we want a profound change in which no one's an absent referent, whether it's marginalized people or discarded animals.

I know I've saved a person's life by starting the hotline for battered women and that I helped get ninety-seven units of low-income housing built that wouldn't have been built without my activism. I know people have become vegan from reading my books. (And when they share this with me, I tell them to make sure they are taking B12!). I know of these successes, but I don't feel comfortable measuring things that way. We have to see our activism as something we are doing because we care about everyone who's marginalized as keenly important, *even if we fail* in our specific activism.

With activism work, all we have to do is start. All you have to do is be the person you are today to get started. The steps you take today help you with whatever develops tomorrow. You do not need to know how to do everything today. You do not need to know everything about nutritional yeast to be vegan or how to read a budget of some entity you're challenging or running. We fail to see how we grow through the decisions we make. We take the steps today, and they strengthen us and deepen us, and we become the person who can take more challenging steps the next day because of what we did today. Activism is a process and not a product. Everything we do is because we believe we are all connected, and that others are worth fighting for; we're teaching ourselves how to be the people we believe ourselves to be.

*Cited Works*

Adams, C. J. (2017). Towards a Philosophy of Care through Caregiving. *Critical Inquiry* 43(4). Pages 765-789: https://doi.org/10.1086/691016

# STACY RUSSO

## Sonya Renee Taylor

The Body Is Not an Apology

www.TheBodyIsNotAnApology.com

—

"I wanted to start a movement in which we are allowed to love ourselves."

*Sonya Renee Taylor started a revolution in radical self-love when she posted a photo of herself in a black corset. The essence behind her courageous post immediately resonated on a global scale. She started a company, The Body is Not an Apology, and later wrote a book with the same title. Sonya Renee is also a nationally-recognized performance poet and speaker. One of the most inspiring aspects of her interview is her courage to act when something feels true to her. Acting on these moments of clarity occurred when she quit her job to become a poet, and again when she later followed the message of* The Body Is Not an Apology *until it became the international social justice movement it is today. Sonya Renee discusses her activist journey and some important concepts connected to her work, including "body terrorism."*

—

I was born in Wilmington, Delaware, although most of my family is from Pittsburgh, Pennsylvania. My parents were teenagers when they had me. My dad was in the Navy, so we moved around a bunch when I was growing up. We probably moved about every two years, until I was ten years old and moved back to Pittsburgh. My parents also got divorced when I was ten.

My family life was pretty interesting. There were a lot of challenges being born to teenage parents. My mother struggled with addiction for most of my youth— from about the time I was ten until I was twenty-four— so she was intermittently in my life. Around the time I turned seventeen, I moved out of a group home that was part of a transitional living program for homeless youth.

### How did you manage the stress of what you faced at such a young age?

The arts have been a huge part of my survival and sanity. I went to a performing arts high school throughout most of my youth, until I graduated. I then went to Hampton University, a historically Black college in Hampton, Virginia, and majored in sociology.

I put myself through school by working a lot of jobs. After graduation, I took a job as a therapeutic wilderness counselor, in which I worked with adjudicated youth who were sentenced to treatment programs. I did that for a year, then went to graduate school to pursue a master's degree in organizational management with a focus in non-profits.

### What other jobs did you do early on?

After the therapeutic wilderness counseling, I started work as a case manager for adults with chronic mental illness while I was attending graduate school. Once I graduated, I worked as the director of the peer education program for an organization focused on HIV prevention for street-based sex workers in Washington D.C. It was while I was working there that I discovered performance poetry and ended up quickly quitting my job to become a poet. I was twenty-seven.

**_Wow! That is quite a change. Tell me more about this._**

I went to a spoken-word event sponsored by a fundraiser for the non-profit at which I was working. My employer asked if anyone wanted to write something for the event, and, being that I was already secretly a writer, I decided I would read a poem on stage there. I did not know it was an open mic, and I instantly fell in love with sharing my own poetry. It was an amazing experience. After not engaging in an arts practice for some time, there was something powerful about being on stage in front of an audience again and sharing something I created.

I went back to my office that night and Googled "open mic," because I wanted to know where else I could go. I started going to open mics every single night. I became completely immersed; luckily, at that time in Washington, D.C., there was a thriving arts scene, so I was able to go to an open mic every night of the week.

About two weeks into my open mic experiences, I met someone who became one of my best friends to this day. She asked if I wanted to compete in a "slam." I didn't know what she meant, so she explained that it was competitive performance poetry and that I could win $300. I competed in my first slam and came in third place. I didn't know that I was competing against national champions, so it turned out that I did really well against people who had been doing this for decades and who were internationally renowned.

From then on, I started competing pretty regularly in slams in my local community. In 2004, I eventually ended up on the Washington, D.C.-Baltimore slam team, which took part in national competitions. My first national competition with them was in St. Louis. This included both a team competition and championship, as well as an individual championship. I ended up winning the national individual title that year. In December of that year, as I mentioned earlier, I quit my job to become a poet. I went on tour and started building my career as a performance poet for about the next thirteen years.

### How does your work as a performance poet connect to the creation of The Body Is Not an Apology?

The connection is very specific. In 2010, while on a slam team in Knoxville, Tennessee, I was with a lot of friends in a hotel room getting ready to compete, and I started having a conversation with my friend, who has cerebral palsy. She felt concerned that she might have an unintended pregnancy. I asked her why she wasn't using protection with her partner, and she very honestly shared with me that, due to her disability, she didn't feel entitled to ask this person to use a condom. I said to her very instinctually, "Your body is not an apology. An apology is not something that you offer to someone for your disability." When I said those words, they felt important to me. They were not just a specific truth for her and her situation. They were important in a general sense. Those words felt bigger than just that one moment. In that moment, the extent of my vision was to write a poem, which I titled "The Body Is Not an Apology," and started performing it around the world.

I believe in the power of language to create and change the world. There was a way in which my act of walking around saying "The Body Is Not an Apology" every day was challenging me to live in it. It was also highlighting all the ways in which I was maybe not in alignment with what I was saying on the stage. This led me to share a selfie that I had been hiding in my phone. Although I felt beautiful and powerful in the photo, I was concerned about what the world might think about it; so, for months. I didn't share it. Then, someone shared a photo on my Facebook page of a plus-sized model named Tara Lynn in a black corset, and I thought she looked beautiful and fabulous. In the photo I hadn't shared, I was also wearing a black corset. In that moment, every-thing came together.

That night, I shared my photo and asked others to share a photo in which they felt beautiful and powerful in their bodies. By the morning, thirty people had tagged me in photos. I decided to make a Facebook page titled "The Body Is Not an Apology." After creating the page, I knew in that moment that I wanted it to be something *big*. I wanted to start a movement in which we are allowed to love ourselves.

*Your vision came true. You absolutely started a movement, and now you have much more than the Facebook page. Let's talk about the evolution and expansion of the movement.*

The Body Is Not an Apology is now a full-scale digital media and education company, in addition to a book. It has been seven years since I posted the selfie and started the Facebook page. By the time that summer hit, the page already had a few thousand people on it. I started to think up projects, which were all based on things that I needed to do to reconcile my own relationship with my body. The first project that The Body Is Not an Apology came up with was called the Radically Unapologetic Healing Challenge 4 Us (RUHCUS) project. It's a thirty-day transformational healing project. I started that project because I would wake up every day and tell people to love themselves unapologetically, yet I had been wearing wigs for decades to hide my hair. I have traction alopecia and was teased as a kid. Because of this, I had a lot of hair shame.

I realized that I couldn't grow my vision while still being a hypocrite about the areas of my own shame. I created a thirty-day project to tackle my biggest fear. I invited my community to support me in trying to break free from this immense fear that I had. I could no longer tell people to love themselves unapologetically and then slap on a wig. I invited around ten friends to my house to participate in a shaving ceremony, in which they helped me shave my head. My biggest fear was tied to a belief that I couldn't be beautiful without hair. After shaving off my hair, my friends placed their hands on my head and spoke a blessing of what they hoped would grow. That is how I launched my thirty days of being bald into the world.

Each day I videotaped myself going through the process of living through this big fear. I invited other people to start their own RUHCUS project, and people around the world started doing them for themselves. They did projects around coming out, healing addiction, letting go of childhood trauma, sexual abuse, and many other forms of shame they did not want to carry with them anymore.

To this day, people still write me to tell me about their projects.

**Tell me about another project you've done.**

The second project we came up with was called "Bad Picture Monday." Every Monday, we encouraged people who followed us on our social media platforms to change their profile pictures to photos they hate. People started doing it and realized the ways in which we get indoctrinated into body shame. This happens in the way we convince ourselves of the certain ways that we should be allowed to be seen, and we get deeply invested in this hyper consciousness of how we look. With this project, every Monday became a chance to flex the muscles around radically loving yourself no matter *how* you looked in an image. The project really challenged the notion of conventional beauty.

The Bad Picture Monday project really took off and was the first of our projects to receive mainstream media attention. The project was covered by *The Today Show* and *MSNBC*. Even the *New Yorker Magazine* did a write-up on it.

**Let's talk about some of the concepts in your work. Can you tell me about "body terrorism?"**

It became very clear to me that there was a way in which we were talking about body image, but there was also a way in which we were talking about something so much bigger. Because I have worked with folks with mental illness and HIV, as well as kids facing problems around race, class, and gender, I've always understood the body as a combination of all of those things. I understood that our relationship with our bodies and the world's relationship with our bodies was not just about self-esteem or confidence. *There is an entire system and structure that benefits some bodies. This system not only oppresses other bodies but enacts violence on other bodies.* These things happen as a result of race, class, sexual orientation, mental health status, gender, disability, and all of these other ways that our bodies show up.

I used the term "body terrorism" for the first time around 2012. I was beginning to have a very clear and deep analysis around race, racism and white supremacy in the world and the ways in which all of that was playing out in our bodies.

Shortly thereafter, Trayvon Martin was murdered by George Zimmerman.

*The Biggest Loser* was one of the highest-rated shows on television. Our responses to bodies that do not fall into our understanding of normal is violent. The ways in which we police bodies and have policed bodies throughout history to either make them be "normal" or to punish them for not being so has always been a function of terrorizing people. It became very clear to me that we were not just talking about people's individual relationships with their bodies. These are systems of oppression. The act of inflicting terror on people's bodies for the purpose of political and economic control is called terrorism. This propagates our self-hatred and asks us to propagate that hatred onto other bodies, acting as a global system of terrorism. If we recognize it as a system and not the function of our individual low self-esteem or a few individual greedy corporations, but part of a larger system of power and control, then we can actually begin to deal with it. It creates an opportunity to engage in more intentional strategies to fight it comprehensively.

***That's a powerful explanation. Have you noticed this extends to aging and the body?***

Aging is certainly one of the areas of oppression. There is a lot of "invisibilized" oppression and shaming surrounding aging. Aging also has so many intersections with other areas of body shame and body terrorism. It's intersectioned with disability and weight, for example. It's also an area with which it is really difficult for us to reckon. I am aging. I am forty-one, and I'd like to think I'm still twenty-two. Aging is definitely one of the places in which I get to practice radical self-love for this body that operates differently from how it used to do so. It doesn't allow me to do the things I used to be able to do when I was twenty-five. Then there are the visible signs of aging. I look in the mirror and think, "Oh, you look old!" There is a personal practice of inquiring whether or not I am assigning judgment to looking old. All of the work that radical self-love is, I get to practice every single day— particularly in the face of aging.

I think some of the issues we have are related to how we, as a society, struggle with mortality. We struggle with death, so aging means struggling with approaching the end of life and the ways in which we try to reconcile with that inevitable reality. Although it is the only guaranteed thing we have on this planet, it's the thing we struggle with the most. Because aging intersects with so many other areas of body shame and oppression, if we were able to deal with ableism, for example, we could gain access to a new way of understanding aging. We are still so mired in this system of body hierarchy and which bodies are more valuable, such as able and thin bodies. We are also taught things through our capitalist system, which is tied to the Puritan work ethic. This, and so much more, makes it very difficult to access the value, the wisdom, and the beauty that inherently exists in aging.

*Do you have any final thoughts on your work that you would like to share?*

There are two things that I feel are important to mention within the context of the work of The Body Is Not an Apology. One is that we are a social justice organization that uses the body and radical self-love as our access to justice. Sometimes people flatten the words "body image" or "body positivity," and this does not get at the root of why The Body Is Not an Apology was created.

It is also important to know that this isn't just my work. There is a team of thirty-two people doing this work in different countries. We have folks in Denmark, Australia, England, Canada, and Spain. It's a movement, it's a company, *and* it's a personal practice. Today, people translate our content into Russian, Portuguese, Spanish, French, and German. There are platforms all over the world that are sharing our content and translating it.

*That is an amazing expansion in a relatively short time. I feel it really speaks to the fact that the message deeply resonates. It gets right to the heart of something that so many people are struggling with; there is also joy present in the work.*

Yes, it is tied to the framework of radical self-love. We speak about all the oppressions, but we also talk about how we love ourselves, which gives us love as a framework for the world. And what isn't joyful about love?

### How do you stay positive with your activism work?

I am not sure if I believe in the need to "stay positive." I believe in being both pragmatic and hopeful. I am honest about the world we have. I am compelled daily to do my part to create the world I desire to see, and I am inspired to hope when I watch the collective power of all of our efforts begin to shift the world, by shifting us. That is what feels true.

STACY RUSSO

## Kate Jessica Raphael

Ultraviolet / KPFA Women's Magazine

LAGAIUltraViolet.Wordpress.com / KPFAWomens-Mag.Blogspot.com

—

"Ultimately, what was most important was living in solidarity with Palestinian people."

*If you tune into the "Women's Magazine" show on Pacifica radio station KPFA in Berkeley on Monday afternoons, you will likely hear the voice of Kate Jessica Raphael. Kate has been the host of the feminist show for thirteen years. A lifelong activist, she has been involved in various actions and movements to eliminate injustice and stand united with those facing oppression. For over thirty years, she has also worked with a collective to publish the queer newspaper Ultraviolet. Kate's activism has also been focused on Palestinian rights. Between 2002 and 2005, she spent eighteen months in the occupied West Bank, living and working in solidarity with the Palestinian people. As a writer, Kate uses fiction to promote social justice issues and has written a Palestine-based mystery series published by She Writes that includes the titles Murder Under the Fig Tree and Murder Under the Bridge. Here, Kate discusses the many facets of her activist life.*

—

I was born in 1959 and grew up in Richmond, Virginia. I didn't know this at the time, but that was the era of massive resistance to desegregation in Virginia. Historically, Virginia was the capital of the Confederacy. My family is

Jewish, and my mom grew up in a community in which hers was one of only two Jewish families. The Richmond Jewish community was sizable, even though Richmond is a heavily Protestant, evangelical town. I believe this had an impact on how I saw myself and was seen by others.

When I was going into the sixth grade, schools were desegregated by court order. Most of the white families fled the school district, either by sending their kids to private school or by moving to the surrounding counties that were not bound by the desegregation order. By the time I was in high school, I went to a school that was about eighty-five percent Black. I think this also had an important effect on me. I had the experience of what it might be like to be in a small minority; at the same time, I was aware of the privilege that I had as a white person. I didn't always feel privileged, but there was a part of me that understood that I had certain advantages because I was white.

I graduated from high school when I was seventeen. I went to Oberlin College in Ohio and received a bachelor's degree in government and history with a concentration in women's studies. My father died of brain cancer the summer between my junior and senior year, so my last year of school was paid for by his veteran's benefits. I had one more year of funding following that, so I went directly to graduate school at UC Berkeley. I studied political theory for a couple of years. However, I took a break and never went back. I finished my master's degree, but not my PhD, which is one of my big regrets.

*I know you've been an activist your whole life. You mentioned growing up in the time of school deseg-*

*regation. Do you have other early memories that led to you becoming an activist?*

A lot of it came from my family, since my parents were very socially aware. They weren't activists, but they did take part in subtle actions. For example, they were part of a group called Housing Opportunities Made Equal (HOME), which was focused on fighting housing discrimination. I grew up with the belief that it is important to stand up for what you believe, even if it is unpopular.

One of my first experiences taking a stand was in high school, when I was the editor of the school newspaper. There was a full-time military recruiter assigned to the school, and he would hang out and take pictures of kids. He wanted us to publish the photos and place a military recruitment ad in the newspaper. I didn't want to do this. because I didn't feel it was appropriate to recruit at our school. This was only a few years after the end of the Vietnam War and Watergate, so this was the era of Woodward and Bernstein, which was formative for my generation. I was very much a pacifist at that time.

My stance became a huge issue, and I got a lot of backlash from the school administration. It became a larger question about whether students had the right to run our own institutions— which, of course, we didn't. They started imposing repressive rules around dress and when we could go to the bathroom. We put a petition together and succeeded with rolling back at least some of the rules.

***With regards to some specific justice work you have been involved with, please share about the mission and history of UltraViolet.***

Let me first explain that there are two *UltraViolets*. One is a liberal feminist newspaper and media organization. We're not that. We're a small, radical, queer newspaper. We have been publishing in some form since 1988. Originally, the newspaper was called *Out,* and it started as a newsletter of a group that I've been a member of since 1986: LAGAI-Queer Insurrection.

LAGAI was originally Lesbians and Gays against Intervention in Latin America and was focused on ending U.S. intervention in Central America. We later did a lot of activism against the two invasions of Iraq and have always been active on Palestinian issues. In the queer community, our activism has been focused especially around racism, sexism, and misogyny. We were also very active in the AIDS movement.

We used to publish the newspaper every other month, but now it's only available quarterly. We have always focused on prisoners and prison issues since the 1980s and early 1990s. It's important to take care of political prisoners and remind people they are still there. A number of Black political prisoners have recently been released, but there are still quite a few in prison. Over the years, LGBTQI prisoners have become the majority of our subscribers. We receive around 100 requests from prisoners to be added to the mailing list between each two issues. Because so many prisoners continue to be added to our mailing list, we decided a few years ago to include articles by prisoners in each issue. They can use the newsletter as a vehicle to communicate with each other and the outside world about what their conditions are like. Most of the articles we print are by queer prisoners.

**It is amazing that the newspaper has been in existence for around thirty years.**

Yes, it's an opportunity for us to reflect deeply on our work and where we see it going. We also want to sometimes challenge people that we're working with around things that we think aren't being addressed well, as well as to recognize and celebrate our victories. There is a need to counter mainstream narratives, as well as narratives that get a certain popularity in the left. For instance, people will trash "identity politics," which is often code for feminism and queer identity issues. The straight, male-led left doesn't think that those issues should be given much importance. We definitely don't agree, so we call them out on that.

A big part of why we have been able to sustain *Ultra-Violet* for so long is that we are mostly self-funded. We recently received a grant from the Resist Foundation for a few thousand dollars, which is huge for us. Resist is a great small foundation that makes it possible for grass-roots groups to do a lot of work that they wouldn't otherwise be able to do.

Almost every newspaper I know that tried to raise their costs through fundraising or subscriptions has gone under. People are not very willing to pay for journalism these days, especially tiny grassroots journalism. It is important to think about this. Sometimes we undervalue our own work and think that, if somebody doesn't want to pay for it, that means it is not worth doing. The honest truth is that some of us are able to spend money going to the movies or on vacations. Why wouldn't we want to spend money to make our world better?

*That is very true and a wonderful way to think about investing in activism work. Let's talk about another big part of your activist life, which is your work related to Palestine. Why did you travel there and how did that become such a significant part of your life?*

Israel and Palestine have always been important in my life because my family was very Zionist. The family members who remain are still very Zionist, meaning huge supporters of the state of Israel. My parents' generation was very much affected by the Nazi Holocaust and believed that having a state was an important means of security for Jews. I didn't really question that growing up; but, as I became increasingly more anti-militarist, I became aware of how Israel served a very self-conscious form of militarism. There was a belief that we were strong because we had the most powerful fighters and fighting equipment. I didn't know anything about the Palestinians, but that aspect of it didn't feel right to me.

When I started college in 1976, the Soweto uprising in South Africa was happening. Even in high school, my friends and I were interested in the South African liberation movement because the students involved were our age. In college, I learned about Israel's role in arming the South African government. I believe this pushed me to think more about Zionism, but I honestly did not want to think about it too much. Then, in 1982— when Israel invaded Lebanon and, eventually, several thousand Palestinians were massacred in refugee camps— it forced many of us to take a stand against the Israeli government. It took me a long time to recognize that it wasn't just about a single bad administration; ultimately, the whole development of colonization in Palestine was a wrong approach to trying to create security for Jews.

Even though I felt strongly about this, I've never really been someone who wanted to live outside of the U.S. I don't learn languages that easily, and I always felt like my work is here on U.S. soil, to affect our own government's policies. This changed when the second Intifada began in September 2000, and the Israeli government attacked nonviolent protestors with a brutality that we had really not seen. It was a large escalation. They fired one million bullets into nonviolent protestors within a week. Shortly after that, I saw a call for international activists outside of Palestine to go there and stand with the Palestinians in the hopes of lessening the violence. It seemed to me like that was something I could do.

I encountered an announcement for a project called the International Women's Peace Service that was looking for people with journalistic skills, nonviolent-direct-action experience, and some understanding of the conflict. I applied and was accepted.

**This sounds like a major change in your life.**

It was a personal watershed moment. I quit a job that I had had for a very long time and gave up my apartment. I spent a good part of two years living in Palestine and participating in nonviolent resistance. I realized that the most important work wasn't necessarily what I thought it was

going to be, including advocacy for prisoners and participating in demonstrations. Ultimately, what was most important was living in solidarity with Palestinian people.
Large amounts of energy are spent making Palestinians
feel that no one knows what is happening and that no
one cares about to them. We were there to say, "Someone
sees and cares. We are going to try and make other people
aware and try to get the rest of the world to care."

*That is a great testament to the power of witnessing
and taking the additional step to tell others about
injustice.*

*Another avenue of your activism is work as a host for
a feminist radio show. How did you get involved in
that form of activism?*

I've been involved with *Women's Magazine* now for thirteen years. It is a feminist radio show on KPFA, which is
a listener-supported station in Berkeley. I think it's the
oldest listener-sponsored station in the country, as I believe it was formed in 1947.

The *Women's Magazine* program began around 2005 after a group in the apprenticeship program at the station
and women working on different shows came together to
work on a specifically feminist program because one did
not exist. There were certainly feminists working on other
shows, but there was no program specifically devoted to
women's issues. The group made a proposal to the station
and were given a slot. Lisa Dettmer, one of the women
who started the show, knew me from my past journalism
and activism work, so she recruited me for a planning
meeting. At the time, I had just come back from Palestine

and was mostly interested in doing pieces about Palestine, so I thought I would do a couple of interviews here and there for them.

In June 2005, I did my first interview, which was with a Palestinian lesbian. She was active in the Palestinian lesbian group Aswat, which was pretty new at that time. I recorded the interview on my own, even though I didn't know anything about radio. After the interview, Lisa showed me the editing software, and I quickly picked up how to use it. After I edited the piece, it was on the air in a couple of weeks. It was a really cool experience. As a writer, it can take many months or years for any project that you're working on to be read by anyone. To be able to do something and have it on the air directly and heard by thousands of people so soon was exciting.

Sometime later, I wanted to do a piece about abortion access in the area, which had been curtailed in ways of which most people were not aware. I recorded and edited the piece, and again, it went on the air. Many people I knew heard it and were like, "Ooh. That was so good!" From there, I just got hooked on radio!

I started out producing pieces, and eventually got involved in producing full segments. A lot of people have left, which tends to happen because we're volunteers, since there's no money. The station has quite a few employees, but they're mainly doing technical work and are behind the scenes. The only on-air people who are paid are working on daily shows, and we're a weekly show. Because of this, we have to do the work for the show in our spare time, and it takes an incredibly long time when you're just starting to do it. It used to take me twenty hours or so to do an hour show. Fortunately, it doesn't take quite that long anymore. When someone who had been carrying a lot of the load was having health problems, she thought the show was going to have to go off the air. I said I would take over being the lead producer for a while. Now there's a cohort of women who are sharing the workload more, which is really great.

A majority of the people that we interview are Women of Color. We try to include a diversity of issues and styles, including cultural programs, political issues, interviewing activists, interviewing people who are doing more mainstream politics, interviewing people who are just doing interesting social work or talking about health issues or spiritual issues. I try to make it solutions-oriented because people get so much information about everything that's terrible in the world, and I think most people, including myself right now, are listening to the radio to get inspired and see what they can actually *do*.

More and more, journalism has become national and even international. People are listening to podcasts all over the world. That is all really great, but it is important to remember that there are fewer and fewer venues for local artists and activists to let people know about what they're doing. We try to be very accessible to people who want to let people know what's happening in our area.

*I know you are also a novelist, and your fictional works are intertwined with your activism. Some people reading this book may be artists and creative people who wish to use their creativity for positive change in the world. How did you go about doing this?*

I came back from Palestine with a thousand pages of journals. I sent some pieces out to friends, and many of them responded with saying, "Oh, you should really write a book!" I love mysteries, but when I had tried to write a mystery before, I had not succeeded. However, right before I left Palestine, I got an idea. I saw a scene that I thought would be a good way for a mystery to start, so I decided to try to use the mystery genre to write something about Palestine. There is a global mystery genre that people like to read to learn about other countries and cultures. I hoped people who wouldn't automatically be drawn to a book about Palestine might read it because they liked mysteries. I've since published two books in my Palestine mystery series.

I believe there's a way I can communicate with people through fiction that is very different than the other ways that I can communicate with people through direct activism. Fiction brings me into contact with a lot of people who aren't activists and who may not know any activists. Therefore, through this work, I'm trying to represent activism in fiction in a way that makes it seem possible to people who maybe don't have that orientation.

***Looking into the future, how do you think your work will contribute to the injustices we see affecting marginalized people?***

That's a very hard question to answer. I think our culture really discourages activism and putting yourself out there to try to make change. I hope my books make people think, first of all, "Hey, activism is something everyone can do, and it can help energize and bring my community together. Maybe I should try it!" Secondly, I hope they realize that it is always right to stand against injustice, even if they don't have a perfect strategy or organization. That's how the heroines in my novels live, and it's how I've always tried to live.

## Michelle Carrera

Chilis on Wheels

www.ChilisOnWheels.org

—

"Love has the power to change our whole life."

*Michelle Carrera started Chilis on Wheels, an organization that provides the poor and homeless with warm and healthful plant-based meals, out of her small New York City apartment. Since its founding in 2014, Chilis on Wheels has expanded to chapters in seven cities throughout the United States, as well as a chapter in Puerto Rico. Michelle discusses her awakening to both animal and human rights; how Chilis on Wheels started with her preparing fifteen meals on a special day in 2014; and how she stays inspired as an activist. Her interview provides a great example of how a grassroots organization can begin with a simple action and an individual's love and commitment.*

—

My early life was very happy and calm. I was born in Puerto Rico, and I was an only child for my first nine years. My mom and my grandmother were both animal rescuers. They would see stray animals by the side of the road and pick them up and foster them until they could find them homes. We also ended up adopting some. My grandmother had horses, and I grew up horseback riding. We were not vegan, but we had this love for animals.

My parents both went to college. My mom studied literature and my dad studied information technology. I was exposed to early technology, including things like cell phones that were called car phones, but they were as large as a briefcase. Books and literature were also part of my childhood. My mom would recite poetry to me. She was an artisan, too. She created pottery. She would take me to work with her, and to artisan fairs.

I lived in Puerto Rico until I was twenty-three or twenty-four. I studied comparative literature in college there. In 2004, I moved to New York City.

### Can you tell me about your journey to veganism and how you became an activist?

When I was about twenty-one, my younger sister brought a rooster home. This was a little baby chick. I've heard that for Easter, some schools in Puerto Rico and also in the Southern United States give out chicks. They may even dye them different colors. It's quite horrible that they do that because kids, of course, are not equipped to care for a live animal, and the animals die. When my sister came home with the chick, my mom started to figure out how to take care of him. The little chick grew up inside the house. Eventually, we put him in the backyard. He knew his name. His name was Piolin, which means Tweety Bird in Spanish.

You could call him, and he would run over or wobble over to you. He liked to cuddle under your arm. He liked to put his head under your arm sometimes, to get you to pet him. I loved him so much and I saw that he was incredibly smart. I saw him as a person. I thought, "I can't eat chicken ever again, because this is a person that's looking back at me." I wondered, "How can we do this? Why don't we eat dogs? He's just as smart as our dog." This led me to think of pigs and cows in the same way. That's how I went vegetarian. This was in 2001.

I had never even heard the word vegan. I searched for vegetarianism online using the old dial-up service, and the first link that came up was actually about veganism. The website provided information about milk and eggs and the meat and dairy industries. I had just been vegetarian for a week and a half to two weeks at this time. I decided to give up milk and all other animal products. Within a couple of weeks, I was fully vegan. This all came about because of my love for a rooster. Love has the power to change our whole life.

### What happened early on with your activism?

For the first four years, I didn't know any other person who was vegan. I started working with a dog and cat rescue. I got very involved, and we started a group in Cabo Rojo, which is a town in Puerto Rico. I would see dogs and cats in abusive situations and experiencing extreme neglect. I started developing what I see a lot in vegans. Unfortunately, because we see so much abuse committed by humans, we start resenting humans for all of the atrocities that they're committing. I became kind of harsh towards people.

I moved to New York in 2004 and started getting involved with all of the groups that were active around that time there. I went to protests as well. This one animal sanctuary was also doing humane education classes, which was really interesting to me. The people there were going to a school in the Bronx, and I enjoyed participating in that. Because I speak Spanish, I would go to the bilingual classes.

Still, at this time, I continued to have a kind of disdain for humans. I started reading books by Steven Wise, and I discovered how primates' DNA is so close to our own. They have the capacity to suffer, so they should be treated just like us. During the course of that reading and realization, I thought, "We should treat each other a little bit better, too, because we don't treat other humans nicely, either. How can we argue that we want animals to be treated just like us when we, among ourselves, do not treat each other kindly?" So, animal rights brought me to human rights. That was my journey.

Around this time, I got a job at an adult literacy organization in New York. I started meeting a whole range of people from different backgrounds. I worked at the agency for six years. While being there, I got involved with other human causes, including volunteering at Planned Parenthood, with an immigration coalition, and other places. It may have seemed that I was spreading myself thin by getting involved with every injustice, but later I realized that was how I discovered that all of these things were connected. With Chilis on Wheels, I was able to merge veganism and human rights and put these connections into action.

**Please tell me about the creation of Chilis on Wheels.**

I started Chilis on Wheels on Thanksgiving Day in 2014. At this time, my son was four years old. I realized that our activist life had only dealt with animals, and I hadn't really exposed him to people or community activism. On Thanksgiving Day, I started looking for a soup kitchen at which we could volunteer. Thanksgiving revolves around food, so I thought it would be a perfect opportunity. I started looking for vegan soup kitchens in New York. Surprisingly to me, there were none. I thought to myself, "Well, I should just make the meals myself and give them out." That's what we did. My little pots in my kitchen were able to make fifteen meals of vegan chili. We went to the street and gave them out to people. It was a very surreal day. It was also the first snow of the season, so it was magical.

This first-time bringing food to people was around 11:00 in the morning. We were in the Union Square area, and there were no cars. It was usually so busy with people everywhere, but no one was around this time. This just added to that level of surrealism. We went to people who were on the sidewalks and offered them a meal. The chili was very warm. We saw people eating really fast; it was the kind of eating that comes from hunger.

This experience hit me really hard. When we were done, I just kept thinking about the other 364 days of the year. I said, "I need to do this a little more often." I thought maybe I could do it once a month. My only plans were for it to be my son and I doing this. When I put the story up on Facebook, friends and family were really encouraging. I remember someone wrote, "I'm going to send you twenty dollars, so you can make a little bit more meals." I wasn't expecting anything like that. So, I did it again next month. Then I continued doing it monthly for about three months. It didn't feel significant because people were really hurting. I started doing it once a week, but I couldn't continue affording it on my own, as a single mother. I was making about fifty meals a week. (After that first time, I had bought bigger pots.)

To be able to do it weekly, I started asking supermarkets for food donations, but they would respond by explaining that I needed to be an official nonprofit for them to be able to give donations. I thought, "Then I'll just do that." Chilis on Wheels received its nonprofit status in 2015. Since then, we have expanded to other cities, and the amount of meals we have been able to provide keeps growing. Right now, we prepare about 100 to 200 meals each week in New York. The communities have gotten to know us. We set up in the park, and the community comes to us. We have other programs, too. We have vegan dog food for homeless people with dogs, because we were seeing that the people would sometimes give the chili to their dogs instead of eating it themselves. We did not want them to sacrifice their own meal for their family.

We also have a Kid's Engagement Program that allows kids to volunteer. We have young volunteers— from two years old and all the way up to teenagers in high school. We also have a vegan education program in which we go to schools, churches, and community centers. Chilis on Wheels focuses on low-income communities because they are not reached enough by mainstream organizations.

In addition to all of this, we offer a community support service through our free store that provides personal care items, such as soap, shampoo, and lotion— all of which are vegan. We've had a lot of requests for sleeping bags, which we try to source. If we don't have something available that is needed, we'll tell the person to come back the next week. We'll then spread this need amongst our community and see who has the needed item to donate for the person. We also have clothing drives every two months.

***That is amazing that all of this started from your small pots and kitchen. I understand you are now living back in Puerto Rico. Can you tell me about the type of work you are doing there?***

I received news of the devastation of Hurricane Maria, which hit Puerto Rico and the Virgin Islands, through online radio stations. I knew I had to go back to Puerto Rico then. I reached out to A Well-Fed World, which is an organization that has supported us since the beginning. They were able to give us a grant, so, eight days later, which was the earliest I could get a plane ticket to Puerto Rico, we were on the ground and preparing vegan food. There was no power, so we were cooking by makeshift fires in parking lots. Within a month, we had served 10,000 meals. We served all day, every day. There was no food in the supermarkets, since the ports had been closed. There were three-hour lines to get into a super-market that already had bare shelves.

Some people were in nursing homes and were too frail to go out and get in these lines. The same was true with orphanages. We started serving those types of establish-ments. This was a time when the government was no-where to be found. It all came down to people helping people. A couple of times, we also went into communities in the center of the island. No one had reached them yet.

We also provided services, such as filtering water. While doing this work, the questions of what relief is and what is rebuilding resonated with me. Dropping in and out without leaving support didn't seem to be enough; in a way, it seemed to me to be even worse! When Puerto Rico was taken off the news cycles and all of these big organizations left, what were people supposed to do? Workers were left without jobs, there was *still* no power, and suddenly, there was no more aid, either.

Throughout the course of delivering these meals, we also saw that people didn't know what veganism was, but they were curious. They had heard the word but weren't sure what it meant; or they knew what it meant but didn't think they could do it. I decided to stay and open up a vegan community center here called *Casa Vegana de la Comunidad*. It's a house that has some space for growing our food. We have a space for screening documentaries. We offer cooking workshops, including ones for children. We go out to communities and serve them vegan meals three days a week. We also have a rescued hen and a rooster who have become spokespersons for their species. Most recently, we just received a grant that will allow us to increase our workshops, including programs related to sustainability and growing your own food.

### How do you stay inspired with your activism?

Mr. Rogers once said, "When I was a boy and I would see scary things in the news, my mother would say to me, 'Look for the helpers. You will always find people who are helping.'" Therefore, to stay inspired, I look at other people who are doing amazing things. We are so bombarded with all of the negative news and horrid things that are happening in the world, and it is easy to go down the route of, "What does it matter?" or "What does any of this matter in the scheme of things?" Yet, when I see other people doing things to help, their commitment is beautiful to me.

I look for the positive news of people working for a better world in whatever field it is. For example, The Pollination Project funds a different project every single day of the year. I love reading their newsletter because it's so inspiring to see what people across the world are doing for their communities, animals, the planet, and their neighbors. It's amazing. That's what keeps me inspired.

I also look at how kids are stepping up. They have so much optimism. It keeps me going. I know someone will come from behind and continue the work that is already being done. I'm going to take it as far as I can and someone younger with more energy and optimism will eventually come and take it a million times further.

STACY RUSSO

## Celeste Chan

Queer Ancestors Project

www.QueerAncestorsProject.org

—

"I wanted more of this queer world."

*Celeste Chan's activism work is intertwined with her creative life as a writer and prolific filmmaker. Her initiatives are inspired by a desire to provide People of Color and trans and queer individuals with safe and supportive spaces that empower them to express themselves through telling their stories. Her projects include DIY Art School, Queer Ancestors Project Writes, Writing Rainbow: QTPoC Free School, the co-founding of Queer Rebels, and her own prolific filmmaking career. In this interview, she discusses her work and the impact of several significant elements that led to her activist life, including family stories, riot grrrl feminist punk subculture, DIY ethos and zinesters, queer culture, and influential books.*

—

My parents met in the Bay Area during the Sixties, while my mother was going to UC Berkeley. My parents attended Free Speech events, anti-war protests, free concerts, and listened to Joan Baez and Joni Mitchell albums. I often wondered what it felt like during that time. I watched videos of the '68 Third World Students strikes and imagined what it was like to seize those megaphones, to demand an education that was relevant and accessible– an education by and about People of Color.

It is tongue-in-cheek that I say I am an artist and writer schooled by Do-It-Yourself culture and immigrant parents from Malaysia and the Bronx. My siblings and I were actually homeschooled in Seattle— before it was legal. My education consisted of biweekly visits to Seattle Public and King Country libraries, and my mom didn't restrict what we checked out. There was no distinction between school and life and no definite sense of "now we're in a classroom" or "time off– no more thinking about school." It all blurred together.

DIY Culture felt immediately comfortable to me because my parents did a lot of things that would be considered "punk" – like shopping at thrift stores, recycling materials, and using the library and newspapers for homeschool assignments. They sort of embodied a DIY spirit.

### When did you become politically awake?

Several moments led up to my political awakening. I grew up hearing fragments of my parents' stories. My father lived in a relocation camp during the Japanese occupation of Malaya when he was six to nine years old. My mother told me she often went to bed hungry while growing up in the Bronx. My siblings and I were lucky. It seems like I always knew this. I knew about suffering and injustice and random luck from an early age. My parents made it through hard times, and I am proud of where they come from and how they dealt with what they have been through. My family– homeschooled, Asian-American, mixed-race, class-jumping– broke unspoken rules. We were one of the few families of color in my neighborhood.

Things later clicked for me when I discovered the band Bikini Kill at the library. I screamed along to "Rebel Girl" and came out at sixteen. Friends pointed me to *This Bridge Called My Back*, Leslie Feinberg's *Stone Butch Blues*, bell hooks' *Feminist Theory: From Margin to Center* and *All About Love*, and I ate it up. I read Randall Kenan's *A Visitation of Spirits*, which is about a Black gay teenager coming into his sexuality through the theory of relativity. There was no turning back.

After attending a Queer Youth Rights meeting– my first exposure to politically-active queer/trans youth, organizing campaigns and planning trips to San Francisco for Young, Loud, and Proud as part of Seattle Young People's Project— I knew I had to jump into the mosh pit of community. I wanted to go to everything. I wanted to stay up all night at raves. I wanted more of this queer world.

My friend Jed took me to Olympia, and I started going to drag shows, secret cafes, mudwrestling, and Ladyfest. I saw *The Transfused*: a rock opera created by Nomy Lamm in collaboration with the Need, about a group of multi-gendered beings finding each other and rising up against corporate rule and greed. I think I went up to Nomy afterwards, stammered "I love you" and then ran away. *The Transfused* inspired me so much.

I read zines like *Bamboo Girl*, which was radical because it was the first time I saw Asian American feminists being in-your-face, unapologetic and fierce, femme, tattooed, and proud. I also read Lauren Martin's *Quantify* and *You Might as Well Live* and found a kindred spirit– the first Chinese-Jewish person I'd talked to outside of family. Her writing about living through depression and on having a mixed-race identity really resonated with me. At this time, I was enthralled with riot grrrl, a third wave feminist movement organized around punk music and art. Mimi Nguyen's zine, *Evolution of a Race Riot*, showed the same oppressions existed in riot grrrl as a microcosm of society. While reading it, I discovered first-hand experiences of racism and classism within the movement. I began to look more for other Feminists of Color, for allies, and for people with both a punk rock attitude and larger, expansive vision of a liberated society. I carried *Race Riot* around for what felt like a whole summer in Portland.

### How did you become an activist?

In 1999, I attended the WTO Protest in Seattle with my girlfriend. Seattle Center was filled with people: marching papier-mâché turtles, families with signs and strollers, anarchists, queer punks, and teamsters. It was the largest protest I'd ever seen. My girlfriend wanted to go right up against the row of riot cops. She stood facing them down while I attempted not to hyperventilate into a paper bag. Then, police started launching tear gas canisters and pelted protestors with rubber bullets. The crowd surged and the streets were thick with people, so it was hard to run, but we got out. The mayor declared martial law, so we couldn't leave the house. I'd see the same images on the news– broken windows at Starbucks– and wondered what else had happened.

At nineteen, I knew I wanted to be an activist, even though I didn't want to stare down a sea of riot cops. As luck would have it, I got laid off from my job, which gave me the impetus to move to Olympia and enroll at Evergreen State College. From 2001 to 2002, I became involved in organizing with Homo a GoGo, which was a queer multidisciplinary arts festival based in Olympia, Washington and run by Ed Varga alongside other organizing committees. It took place in 2002, 2004, and 2006, and moved to San Francisco for its last festival run in 2009.

During my time there, I worked on the film committee. Our film lead fell ill, so I agreed to help host the screening with my friend Elliat. We were nineteen and twenty-two, and just winged it! We didn't know what we were doing, and there was no rehearsal. However, we managed to introduce filmmakers and their films, stalled during technical difficulties in the program, and jumped up and down like weird art cheerleaders. The experience was exhilarating and showed me that all you really need to create change is a few people, time, and commitment. You can start a festival from the ground-up or a free library, zine archive, printmaking project, punk feminist tour, or an international Queer art gathering– whatever you want and need– and create it with enough people and enough commitment and resources.

I remember seeing those few blocks of downtown Olympia transformed by throngs of freaky queer people and artists of all types, from as far away as Berlin, Vancouver, and San Francisco. After that, I knew that I wanted to immerse myself in art as activism; and I wanted a community with which to do so.

**Is this how you became involved with your work under Queer Rebels?**

I co-founded Queer Rebels in 2008, with my then-partner KB Boyce. Queer Rebels is a manifestation of art as activism, of curatorial activism— of critical connections between People of Color. We had been talking about how there should be a platform to promote and support queer and trans artists of color, so we started with Queer Rebels of the Harlem Renaissance, which emerged from KB's Drag King of the Blues performances. Our mission was to showcase queer artists of color, connect generations, and honor our histories with art for the future. We debuted our first show in the National Queer Arts Festival with a $500 grant and fourteen artists. We thought it would be a one-time event, but after seeing the standing-room-only crowd, we had to continue. I think that helped give it momentum.

Queer Cultural Center became our fiscal sponsor. We applied for more grants, built a website, took Boot Camp for Artists, and we were off! We kept building and received more funding, which allowed us to create new programs. We created SPIRIT: A Century of Queer Asian, Arab, and Pacific Islander Artivism; and Queer Rebels Fest, bringing in all genres and People of Color from diverse backgrounds.

One project in particular, which I'm really excited about, is our films program. Queer Rebels launched our film program in 2012, partnering with MIX NYC Queer experimental film festival and OUTsider fest. I served as the film curator. I loved curating experimental and boundary-pushing Queer and Trans of Color videos because so often, People of Color are forced to constrict ourselves– to be legible, to be respectable, to not be too weird. I'm most drawn to work that combines urgency with experimentation.

We curated programs such as *The Fight for Home* that features Persia, a Latina drag queen in heels standing in front of a red-dotted map of evictions, screaming "Stop being poor" to a San Francisco museum audience. Persia collaborated with DADDIE$ PLA$$TIK to create "Stop being poor"– tackling classism and capitalism in the vein of their famous anti-gentrification anthem, "Google google apps apps." In Kevin Simmonds's *ORIENT*, Black and Asian communities come together in the struggle for racial justice after the LA riots. *Viet Le* shows that home is displacement through a transtastic Ha Noi music video/visual poem on the 40th anniversary of the Vietnam War. In Cosmo Soltani's *Dessert Lullabies*, a seven-year-old girl flees war in Iran, escaping into a night of ancestral fairytales with the spirit of her deceased grandmother.

There are invisible threads weaving our lives together. The language of racism is violence– through police brutality and state violence, through war, through poverty. James Baldwin said it best: "The place in which I'll fit will not exist unless I make it." I think that is the biggest thing that inspired Queer Rebels: that want of community; a space for weird, freaky artistry; and QTPoC movement building.

I stepped down from the company in 2018, after ten years of service. One of the artists, Crystal Mason, stepped up to become managing director. The time had come for me to do something else. I had already launched Queer Ancestors Project Writes and Writing Rainbow:

QTPoC Free School. It was time for me to delve deeply into my own work— particularly my writing.

***Your passion as a film curator for Queer Rebels and your excitement for films is contagious. Can you tell me some more about how filmmaking became part of your activist life?***

I first learned about filmmaking from Evergreen State College's International Feminism course. This multidisciplinary course— taught by Angela Gilliam, Ju-Pong Lin, and Terese Saliba— touched on literary theory, international relations, art installations, video production, creative writing, and feminist and queer theory. Angela Gilliam, who passed away earlier this year, was my mentor. She pushed me to learn how to speak up in class. I was really shy up until that point. Evergreen was all about student dialogue in seminars, and this openness really helped me. I grew up in alternative education, and International Feminism encapsulated everything that I wanted to study. I wanted a school at which you could get credit from life-learning; a school in which students were active in co-creating the classroom.

My documentary roots came from Evergreen. I earned my BA in International Feminism. I was not a film major, but, inspired by riot grrrl/DIY feminist ethos, I learned basic video production, and then continued to teach myself hands-on filmmaking by borrowing the school's equipment and taking a film class after graduation.

My first films were experimental documentaries— and I keep making them! I'm in the process of completing *Artists of a Riot* (formerly *ART Heart: Children of Riot Grrrl and Queercore*), my longest work to date. Much of my work explores themes of migration and displacement, trauma, family histories, race, class, gender, and sexuality. For my film *Malaysian Memories*, I interviewed my Chinese immigrant father on how he survived the Japanese occupation of Southeast Asia.

My film *ABSENCE: No Fat, No Femmes, No Asians* featured interviewee Esther Kim speaking about the intersections of racism/classism/sexism/and size discrimination, alongside images of empty stages and rows of lipstick resembling armor. *Queer Historical Mixtape*, commissioned by Radar Productions and created in collaboration with artist Irina Contreras, used clips from the GLBT Historical Society Archives. In this documentary, a transgender woman in high heels and red fringe dress dances to Tina Turner, while Dorothy Allison's voice says, *When you heal the broken places, you put some real muscle into it. Work is salvation.*

A couple of years ago, I created a solo show called *(Re)generation*. It weaves stories from my parents and grandparents experience of World War II, which I tied together through experimental film. While the stories delve into atrocities, I chose not to dwell there. I'm more interested in war's aftermath: it's psychological lingering, the ghosts it leaves behind; what does one do with a haunting? What histories do we inherit and what do we create? Those are the questions I hope to answer as I expand *(Re)generation* into a manuscript.

**Tell me about some of your other projects, like the MFA/DIY Art School.**

I left an MFA program after hearing "this isn't universal enough" and "real art is beyond small press writing by whatever oppressed minority group you identify with." I decided to create an MFA-like experience outside of school by taking a series of community writing classes. In between that, I went back to school for a MSW degree. San Francisco State's program was majority People of Color, and many of the students worked fulltime while earning their degrees. I ended up working and volunteering at almost all of SF's domestic violence/anti-violence hotlines– SFWAR, CUAV, W.O.M.A.N. Inc., and the Riley Center. I had a long social work career before transitioning into grant writing and education.

In late 2015, I joined DIY MFA (a.k.a. DIY Art School). Under threat of legal action from a for-profit LLC, we changed our name to DIY Art School. Inspired by Freedom Schools during the Civil Rights Movement, homeschoolers, and Evergreen State College's alternative education, we wanted to hack capitalism and create our own community-driven arts education. We took turns facilitating lessons, did in-home student visits, presented works in progress, and talked about art shows and performances that we could attend. This all inspired me to launch Writing Rainbow: QTPoC Free School.

I often wondered– what *is* an MFA? It includes craft and theory lessons, time, commitment, a creative cohort, and community. What if you could create your own cohort? What if it were a generous space– supportive of identity and experience, framed around generosity towards other writers?

Launched in 2016, I wanted Writing Rainbow to specifically support Queer and Trans People of Color– both students and teachers. It started smaller; I thought I would teach all of it but that was just too ambitious. I wanted to hear from other writers and other teachers in this specifically QTPoC space. Now, it is a series of workshops lead by QTPoC artists and teachers, which I coordinate.

## Is this what led to the Queer Ancestors Writes project?

Yes, although Queer Ancestors Project (QAP) Writes is different. Whereas I coordinate Writing Rainbow, in QAP Writes, I develop LGBTQ-focused creative writing curriculums to teach the 30-week/9-month-long program. I'm jumping ahead, though. Let me tell you how I got started with QAP.

I'd admired Queer Ancestors Project for years. Founded and directed by artist Katie Gilmartin, the Queer Ancestors Project printmaking program had been going strong since 2010. I'd been to their print shows over the years and had also been invited as a guest artist to show films and discuss my work with Queer Rebels. When I saw there was a funding opportunity through WritersCorps, I approached Katie with the idea of collaborating and launching QAP Writes. She was enthusiastic about the idea, so we worked on the grant together, and it came through. QAP Writes launched in September 2017.

It was challenging and amazing; it was completely life-changing! I *loved* creating curriculums from scratch. Lessons ranged from cut-up poetry to cut-up revisions. I had students read Justin Torres's essay "In Praise of Latin

Night at the Queer Club," written in the aftermath of the Pulse Orlando shooting; and then watch Sylvester singing "You Make Me Feel Mighty Real" under disco lights. Sometimes, I would send students on scavenger hunts to engage their senses, and they did everything from sit in a giant plush heart to write or trace colors in a glow-in-the-dark room.

I enjoyed pairing contemporary and historic writers, and it just made sense. For example, I paired Gloria Anzaldua with her mentee, Meliza Banales (who came to speak to the youth and blew them away), James Baldwin's letters and Arisa White's poetry, and Leslie Feinberg's *Transgender Warriors* with Cheryl Dunye's *The Watermelon Woman*. We also read Cherrie Moraga's *The Last Generation* and Kai Cheng Thom's *Fierce Femmes and Notorious Liars: A Dangerous Transgirl's Confabulous Memoir*.

I'm proud that we collaborated with Foglifter Press to publish our anthology: *Tender: Queer Ancestors Project Anthology*, featuring creative writing and prints from QAP students. In the anthology, Sylvia Rivera compels us to stay and fight, speaking to poets "becoming trans femme." Guan Yin offers queer elegies, poems to transform trauma from friends fallen to suicide. We also have serpent women, genderqueer mermaids, and glitter crusted love found in the sea, sky, and clubs to queerly remind us of our community's defiance, beauty, survival, and creativity. Declarations of self-love combat silence, and the real-life struggles of poverty, isolation, migration, and homo/transphobia.

Can QAP Writes be a space to transform isolation? I want queer and trans youth to know that queer culture is

itself a history of resistance - from lesbian feminists starting presses at their kitchen tables in the 1980's (thanks,
Kitchen Table Press) to the original Stonewall and Compton's Cafeteria riot queens – we, LGBTQ people, have
such a rich history of art and cultural resistance. Young
people have told me that "there's so few spaces to explore our history, specifically as Queer and Trans Youth
of Color." I'm proud to work with Katie. It's a supportive
community space, a classroom where students feel empowered to pursue their creative interests. As student Jose
Francisco says in his poem "Rise," *we hold the power to shape
the future, and, together, to shake these walls down.* I feel hopeful.

**The amount of work you have completed in a short
time is astonishing! What keeps you going like this?**

I love the act of creation. I love creating projects from the
ground-up. After being a deeply depressed and closeted
teen, I believe in transformation through the art and
community spaces we both create and need to see. I had
to do something with my anger and energy, to reach out
and resist by every means. Faced with ongoing depersoni-
fication – anti-transgender legislation, hate crimes, ICE
raids, church/mosque/synagogue/school shootings, police murders of unarmed Black people, immigrant detention and child separation at the border, the Pulse Orlando
shooting – we need community, we need our stories, we
need to be reminded of what we are capable of. We need
to be visible, to continue creating, to be in conversation
with each other. We need more connections. We need to
know the histories that we come from.

I'm here because my parents and grandparents survived. Like Edwidge Danticat, I believe that we are here to "create dangerously, for people who almost didn't exist."

# Helène Aylon

Artist

www.HeleneAylon.com

—

"At that moment, I knew I was certainly a feminist."

*In Helène Aylon's autobiography* <u>Whatever is Contained Must be Released: My Jewish Orthodox Girlhood, My Life as a Feminist Artist</u> *(Feminist Press), she documents her long career as a feminist artist and activist. It was after her youngest child was in kindergarten that Helène started her pursuit of an art degree, which she considered "a degree in freedom." Her career has traveled through three phases: the body in the 1970s, the earth in the 80s, and God (G-D) in the 90s to the present. At age 88, she continues to create art with a feminist consciousness. Helène is represented by the Leslie Tonkonow Gallery in New York City. Herein, she discusses her journey as an activist artist, including some of her influential and large-scale performance pieces.*

—

I was born in the Jewish ghetto of Brooklyn known as Boro Park and grew up within Orthodox Judaism. My father was a business man, while my mother was a supreme homemaker. I was the oldest of three girls. My upbringing was a rather conforming situation, except somehow, I managed to grow up to be a non-conformist.

When I was around twelve, down the block from me, there were two older and very pretty teenage girls who would sit on the porch and draw. They were not part of my Orthodox community and seeing them create art was very thrilling. It seemed like a wonderful thing to be able to do. It was an early experience of seeing art-making.

**You were around thirty when you started to follow your dream of being an artist, correct?**

Yes, I was around that age when I started to pursue it seriously. I was engaged at seventeen, married young at eighteen. I had my first child at nineteen and then had another baby soon after. It was when my youngest child, my daughter, was in kindergarten that I managed to get into Brooklyn College. I saw getting a degree in art as a degree in freedom. Getting out of a structured existence was freeing. Getting away from the people I knew and just being with others was also freeing to me. I thought it was a big thing to finally get to a place in my life and work and actually declare myself an artist. One needs to declare oneself. Nobody will do it for you.

I studied art with Ad Reinhardt. He did not really teach, which I liked. I had more freedom to do what I wanted. He would look around and mumble something and let me be, which I appreciated. I didn't want any rules or regulations about art. I still feel this way. If a teacher recognizes something intrinsic in a student, then it may be more valuable to let the student produce than to teach an idea that emanates from the teacher's own experience.

**You state that art gave you freedom. Then, you found feminism, which is, of course, intertwined with your artwork. In your book you wrote, "My salvation arrived in the form of feminism." Please tell**

*me about this.*

Absolutely. Feminism saved my life. We all have many experiences that lead to becoming a feminist, right? We may have a history of feeling upset and distraught about a sexist remark and we feel our "dis-ease," as Mary Daly would say, since these remarks, including those that downplay women's achievements and belittle women, are like inhaling bad air. That's the disease of sexism. Its adverse effects put us at our "dis-ease." You experience situations in which you are obstructed, or you are prevented from going to the next level.

I had a great moment of awakening to feminist consciousness when I was in Shabbat in Berkeley in the early 1970s. I was around age forty. I had stopped going to the synagogue by this time, and some friends asked me to please go with them. I consented, and, when I arrived, I felt rather nostalgic. When the candles were lit for the ceremony, it brought everything back that was positive, including the lighting of the candles, which represented the feminine to me.

I quickly hid behind the curtain. Eventually, I peered slightly from behind and saw the men attending Shabbat huddled in an exclusive way, since men and women are not permitted to sit together during prayer services. When I saw them together like that, suddenly, in that moment, something came to me in a salient manner, and it struck me. At that moment, I knew I was a feminist. Seeing the men being exclusive and huddled together created a divided feeling inside me. It was a disparaging situation to be in as a Jewish person, because I loved the feeling of the Sabbath; but, at that moment, I realized I was being restricted and relegated to a certain position because I was a woman.

*In some ways, your break from traditional religion reminds me of how you also went beyond conventional means with your art practice. At a certain point, you let go of what we could call traditional artist materials, such as paints or brushes, and you returned to the earth in the form of sand. What was this process like?*

In the 1970s, I started painting very elusive silver works that could be seen in different ways due to the two layers of Plexiglas I used. Depending on the light source and the angle of the position, the work would appear differently. Around 1981, I began thinking in different ways about my art. It was that year when I did an installation at the Women's Building of San Francisco, where I covered the whole auditorium floor with sand– like a beach. Beneath the sand were five-foot-long squares of muslin, which you couldn't see. The muslin covered the floor, like carpet. Around 500 women came, and most of them sat on the sand. There was a balcony for those who didn't sit but wanted to watch. I performed this piece with Anna Halprin, a choreographer/postmodern dancer; and Pauline Oliveros, a new age musician. I said, "Feel beneath you where you're sitting and reach for the muslin and make a sack of sand and carry it out." There was an exodus from the building as all of the sand was carried out. It took hours! Pauline Oliveros played a recording of crickets. We, the carriers, were asked to hum as we carried out our "burdens," which were represented by the sand. If the burden got too heavy, we were asked to say "ah." So, there was this duet between the human sounds and the crickets as the carriers went out of the building. Anna Halprin led the exodus, like a procession or a dance.

Some people were alone, while some people participated in groups or with a partner. Some tied the sacs tightly with double knots, and some let the sand drip out. I was not yet that political, but this led to my becoming an activist and my *Earth Ambulance* installation.

I used the image of a sac in my work for a long time, in opposition to the military's Strategic Air Command (SAC). In my work, the sac was something that could change and be used for many purposes. I created *Stone sacs* as a performance piece when I went to Israel and Lebanon and worked with Arab and Jewish women. We gathered stones together to put in "sacs." We didn't speak about politics; we talked about ourselves, about menstruation, and other things like that that made us individuals in one another's presence. It was peaceful and brought us together in that moment, despite real-world conflicts between our communities. After this, I created *Earth sacs*, which were pillowcases that I filled with earth "rescued" from twelve military sites all over the country.

During this time, I had just moved to Berkeley and heard Dr. Helen Caldicott, the physician and anti-nuclear activist, speak at UC Berkeley. I remember she said, "Wherever you are in your life, you must think about the future. Use your imagination." When I thought about my own work, I thought, "How does my work affect everything else?"

I decided that I was going to do something to stop the military. I put a small ad in the newspaper, saying, "I am going to go to SAC sites across the U.S. I am an artist and I want to do something about nuclear proliferation and the military." I received responses from eleven women who wanted to come along with me on this trek across the country. In 1982, I created what I called an *Earth Ambulance.* At this time, I was teaching a class that I had proposed as "Performance Art as Anti-War Strategy" at the Feminist Institute in Berkeley and recruited some of my students for this installation

I asked the women to bring their pillowcases and write their dreams and nightmares on them. Some wrote personal intentions, such as "I fear for my children's children." Others wrote about terrible experiences they had with sexism and other horrors, including sexual assault. I was surprised by what was written. Because of the intent of the *Earth Ambulance,* I thought the writings would be about war and nuclear weapons. Through their writings, you could see how everything is connected in that all of these horrors— including sexual assault, sexism, and nuclear proliferation— were connected to the patriarchy.

We traveled to the SAC sites in the *Earth Ambulance* and filled the pillowcases with the soil that we dug up near the bases. The *Earth Ambulance* was a truck I rented for about one month. I covered it with white contact paper and painted a red cross on it. I wrote "Earth Ambulance" on the truck in black. After visiting the twelve sites, the pillowcases were brought to the United Nations in New York City in the *Earth Ambulance.* We then emptied out the pillowcases at "The Isaiah Wall," which is located across from the U.N. The pillowcases were then hung up along the Dag Hammarskjold Plaza on 47th Street, between First and Second Avenue. It was magical to see all of the pillowcases hanging with the dreams and nightmares written on them.

I also started receiving pillowcases from all over the world, including the peace camp in Comiso, Italy, as well as Greenham Common in England, so I was moved to go back to the U.N. a year later to hang more pillowcases. I ended up exhibiting the pillowcases on the facades of three major museums. One was at the Berkeley Museum for the 50th anniversary of Hiroshima and Nagasaki. In 2006, I hung all the pillowcases at the American University Museum in Washington, DC. As an artist, I had now become focused on being an activist.

In 1985, I had gone to Japan for the 40th anniversary of Hiroshima and Nagasaki. I asked Hibakusha (survivors) to write their dreams and nightmares on their own pillowcases, in their own language, and in their own homes. I also spoke at Seika University about feminist art and asked the students to make two large sacs to float in the water. We put seeds and earthly ingredients in the sacs and had them float down the waterfalls on their way to Hiroshima and Nagasaki. One went to Hiroshima and one to Nagasaki. The seeds represent something for the future and implied growth and resuscitation. Some of the students in the class stood on bridges with ropes around their waists ready to jump in to rescue the sacs in case they sank or got caught on a rock. Miraculously, the two sacs did not sink. I remember one student saying to me that if the sacs did not sink, neither would the planet.

For the 75th anniversary of Hiroshima and Nagasaki, I will reveal the contents of the *Seed sacs* from the 40th anniversary.

*When you mentioned you are preparing for a show based around the contents of the sacs, it made it clear that you are still active with your art. At 88 years old, what are you working on or planning?*

It's annoying to be so old, really. Worrying about health issues can be hard, but I get invigorated. I feel invigorated talking about all of this right now. I still try to do a lot. I can divide my long career into three words. The words are "body," "earth," "G-D." In the 1970s, it was the body of the land and the body itself. I created *Paintings That Change in Time* that alluded to the changes of the body and the body being visceral. It is not the *Playboy* image of the body. I saw the body of the land as female. Through the land, I heard the echoes of my foremothers who were left out of history. My career became focused on the earth, which I described through the performance pieces that used sand, stones, earth, and seeds. As for my theological feminism, I focused on the *Old Testament* being very militaristic and misogynistic. That's when I did the whole *G-D Project*, which has been over twenty years long.

*The Liberation of G-D* is one part of the *G-D Project* I did from 1990-1996. We have witnessed the formation of different movements: nonhuman animal liberation, LGBTQIA+ liberation, women's liberation, etcetera, but whatever G-D is, the concept of liberation from it, had not been discussed. G-D had only been spoken for by the patriarchy. I went over every word of the *Old Testament*. I covered the pages with transparent parchment, and I highlighted every word that was disturbing to me in pink. I did not tell anybody what to think. I highlighted what I thought should be evident to people without openly telling anyone what to think. This installation was exhibited in various museums, including the Warhol Museum. The museum curated an exhibit that lasted a whole year called *The Word of G-D,* and it included a solo exhibition of individuals representing different religions. I was chosen to represent Judaism.

At 88 years of age, I'm still very conflicted because I like certain aspects of Judaism. I can get nostalgic at the mystical level, usually when it relates to feminist Judaism. My mother was very Orthodox. I would tell her, "Mom, I do know better than Moses. It's not his fault. He didn't have feminist consciousness." She thought I would be happier if I belonged, but I never really belonged there. When I got very sick and was in a coma for twenty days in 2006, I decided I couldn't pray to that G-D when I came out of it. I had too much resentment to the patriarchal G-D. I didn't know who to pray to, so I decided to go to nature. I went to trees, water, bark, and rocks. I called personal photographs of these experiences *Turnings.*

*I read in your book about some of the other work you did related to women's bodies within the **G-D Project**. Are you continuing your work with the G-D Project? What do you think has been a way that the work you have done has helped continue conversations around Judaism and feminism?*

I'm doing something now that is an off-shoot of the *G-D Project.* I haven't shown it yet. It's called *Headboards,* and it includes Talmudic sexual advice for women. I think it is hilarious. It is advice on sex from Talmudic scholars and includes things such as the frequency of relations, which according to the Talmud laws, depend on one's occupation. If you're a camel driver, it's every six months. If you're a donkey driver, it's every two months. If you're a Talmudic scholar, it's every Friday night or something like that. They actually say this! It is so funny.

In bringing this piece to light, I feel that it is showing that we have come a long way and now know better than past generations of people before us who didn't have feminist consciousness. This consciousness is changing culture, which continues to change the values of society.

# Julia Feliz Brueck

## Sanctuary Publishers / Consistent Anti-Oppression

www.SanctuaryPublishers.com / www.JuliaFeliz.com

—

"We can all make an impact where we are with what we have."

*Julia Feliz Brueck, a published author and illustrator, is a consistent anti-oppression animal rights activist who creates work that brings awareness to various forms of oppression and injustice. In 2017, she founded Sanctuary Publishers as a platform to raise the voices of all marginalized communities through writing. Part of the mission of Sanctuary Publishers is to publish "much-needed content to help make the world a sanctuary for all marginalized communities, and above all, nonhuman animals." Julia is the author and cover illustrator of* Baby and Toddler Vegan Feeding Guide *and the editor of both* Veganism in an Oppressive World: A Vegans of Color Community Project *and* Veganism of Color: Decentering Whiteness in Human and Nonhuman Liberation, *all published by Sanctuary Publishers. She is also the author and illustrator of the children's book* Libby Finds Vegan Sanctuary *(Vegan Publishers, 2016), as well as the illustrator for the children's book* Wild and Free *(Sanctuary Publishers, 2018). Julia discusses her journey to veganism, the creation of Sanctuary Publishers, and her philosophy of activism.*

—

I was born and raised in Puerto Rico. My mom moved us to Florida when I was about twelve, and I lived there until

I was twenty-three. I graduated from Florida Atlantic University with a double major in marine science and art. They had an amazing program with Harbor Branch Oceanographic Institute, and I lived on the research campus, where I was able to take part in different forms of marine science exploration, for about six months. I also met my future life partner there. He is German and was in the U.S. working as a Post Doctorate fellow when his work visa ran out a year into our dating. As he headed back to Europe, he asked me if I would consider moving there, and I agreed. A few months later, I joined him in Ireland, where his new place of employment was located. While there, I completed my master's degree in conservation ecology. After living in Ireland for over five years, we relocated to Switzerland, where we have lived for over seven years. I can confidently predict that this will not be our last move.

### Please tell me about your journey to veganism.

I've been vegan for over a decade now; although I tend to say that I had vegan tendencies before I even knew what that meant. It was always in my nature to care for non-humans as much as humans. In college, I tried to become a vegetarian, and I even joined an animal rights group; but it sort of just didn't click at the time. The group was very focused on food and not on discussing the actual connections of "why vegan," so I really didn't get any awareness about the issues surrounding animal rights. I honestly thought the group was weirdly obsessed with food, and eventually stopped going. (I realize now they were just as excited as I get when new vegan products make it to the market!)

A few years later, I worked and lived with a vegan during my first job after college. This was the first time I consciously heard the term "vegan" itself. However, I still didn't really understand much about why she was vegan (this was before the age of continuous internet access, and we actually lived and worked in a swamp, which made it even more difficult to access information), as she wouldn't speak about being vegan in a work setting. Some of our co-workers would make fun of her when she politely declined to eat the meat and other animal-based foods served at our events. I think that added further to my confusion over what vegan even was. Still, I kept making connections on my own, even if slowly, since I was interested in reducing what harm I caused in the world. I knew I cared about non-human animals and was opposed to cruelty against them; at the same time, I was also concerned about human rights issues and the environment. My love of wildlife and preserving ecosystems was why I had gone into biology in the first place.

It all finally came together when I moved to Ireland. One day, I started watching a film on YouTube that horrified me called *Earthlings*. I was in shock. It wasn't until the reality of what my choices were supporting was put right in front of my face that the veil was ripped off, and I went vegan without another thought.

### How did veganism become a part of your activist life?

My activism and my veganism have changed quite a bit through the years. First, I wanted to scream out to the world and tell everyone I could, "Oh my gosh, this is horrible! This is happening!" I am still horrified, but I realize that not all people have witnessed the same things that I have, and still may have that veil that I did, shielding them from having to face or to admit what they are supporting. When I think back on my journey before going vegan, I can see that people come to awareness at different times. I still speak about veganism, of course; but much of how I go about it is by being an example and focusing on root issues, as well as on intersecting oppressions, which are also influenced by speciesism.

While living in rural Ireland, my activism started by wanting to reach out to other vegans. I started a local group, and I contacted the Vegan Society. I put up posters and made contacts with one other vegan and some vegetarians. Later, I started collaborating with a group from Dublin called The National Animal Rights Association. The person who founded the association helped me establish my activism. I started hosting events. I organized vigils and different types of protests; what I found most impactful in my outreach, though, was tabling. I approached our local health food store about donating vegan food to use as samples, along with homemade baked goods and literature about "why vegan." In these situations, I saw that a lot of people were interested in learning more, and tasting the food made them realize that plant-based food is just as good as nonvegan food. In my mind, my activism was helping people make the connections and understand the impact of their choices, showing them that there is another way. While in Ireland, I also worked with animal sanctuaries and used my writing and drawing abilities to support them and other nonprofits around the world.

Eventually, we moved to Switzerland, which meant my

locally-focused activism came to an abrupt stop. I was in a new country, and I could not speak the local language. In a way, I became isolated. This is when my activism started becoming more individualized. At this time, I also switched to a more digital platform for my activism. I started writing more for different blogs and finding projects that I could do on my own, such as knitting nests for rescued wildlife. In some ways, my activism slowed down; but being isolated also gave me an opportunity to explore the different kinds of activism that were out there and to focus more on my writing and illustration work.

Then I had my first baby.

### How did having your first child influence your activism?

When my son was nine months old, I started taking art classes again, which is how I arrived at the idea for my first book. It is the first-ever vegan-themed board book for babies and toddlers. I made the book with my first son in mind. In my search for ways to teach him about veganism and sanctuary and what those words means, I realized there really wasn't anything like that for very young children. Most books for babies and toddlers normalize nonhuman animal exploitation in farms, zoos, or circuses, and that was really frustrating to me. Around this time, my mom helped rescue a turkey in Florida. I got involved by asking a sanctuary at which I had volunteered if it would help my mom with rehoming the turkey. I started thinking of how I could help more once the turkey was at the sanctuary; this is when the idea for the book and raising money through book sales came to me. The book itself follows the story of Libby (short for Animal Liberation), her rescue, and then her journey to a sanctuary, where she finds safety for the rest of her life. Named after the real turkey that my mom rescued, the book is titled *Libby Finds Vegan Sanctuary*. It took a while, but eventually, I was able to get support for the book and get it published.

I realized through this experience that I had gathered all of this knowledge and I could do publishing on my own. I spoke with my husband about it, and he supported my idea. This was all pretty spontaneous. We were not rich, so I used the tools that I already had, including my skills as a writer and illustrator, to start putting more content out there. This is what I always wanted to do with my work: use my skills as an artist and writer to support nonhumans and other oppressed people. So, in March 2017, Sanctuary Publishers was founded.

**Please tell me what you have worked on in the first year of establishing Sanctuary Publishers.**

The first book I published under Sanctuary Publishers was the *Baby and Toddler Vegan Feeding Guide*. After my first baby was born, I wanted to publish a short, to-the-point resource that would be supportive of new vegan parents. There is so much pseudoscience and misinformation out there that can be dangerous. With this project, my background in research and science came through to create an evidence-based guide, which parents can use to access the information they need as quickly as possible and also to help them if their families or health professionals have questions about raising vegan babies and toddlers.

The proceeds from this guide support the vegan organization Chilis on Wheels. Through Sanctuary Publishers, I am able to both invest money into new books and give back to the activist community. Everything is on a cycle of creating and giving back that sponsors itself through the book sales– at least, that's the plan! Through this work, I am trying to raise the voices of nonhumans and also People of Color, who are often silenced.

**What was the inspiration behind the book *Veganism in an Oppressive World: A Vegans of Color Community Project?***

Before starting Sanctuary Publishers, I was spending time online in spaces for only People of Color. I realized there was this defensiveness when anyone mentioned veganism. I started realizing that People of Color were really put off by mainstream veganism and how it often excuses and tolerates racism, xenophobia, and other forms of oppression. I began working on an idea for the book from that.

I think many people have questions and are unsure what to do or say within these contexts: both white vegans and Vegans of Color. So, this book became a step-by-step guide for mainstream veganism on how to effectively help the movement evolve into one that is consistent in its anti-oppression stance, while providing a resource for Vegans of Color to help white vegans understand how they keep us from the movement and turn People of Color off the vegan "message." There are so many Vegans of Color, but you would never know from the lack of representation.

Creating the book was an amazing learning opportunity for me as well. I learned so much from different cultures and how the experience of veganism varies. Ultimately, I believe mainstream veganism does not realize how invalidating it can be to Communities of Color. Unfortunately, the movement is currently centered on the most privileged humans (white, cis, able-bodied, and male) and currently sends out a message that issues faced by Vegans of Color, such as racism, are not important; yet we are still expected to show up at protests with the risk of facing discrimination and even violence for the color of our skin.

This is why I started speaking out about consistent anti-oppression in veganism and in the way I see us all addressing social justice as a whole. We can't fight injustices if we are adding to the oppression of others while doing it. It's counterproductive to fight for one group while ignoring the plight of others. It doesn't make sense to try to destroy one form of supremacy without also addressing all others, since they are all tied to one another and especially given that so many of us are affected by intersecting oppressions. To add to this, not only do nonhumans face their own injustices, but they are all too often used as tools of oppression against marginalized groups— to "otherize" them. A hierarchy exists in which white supremacy places humanness and whiteness at the very top, followed by People of Color and other marginalized groups; then, at the very bottom, we find nonhuman animals. That human-nonhuman divide, even though we are also biologically animals, is one of those "tools" used when those at the top want to depersonify (i.e. dehumanize) a specific group of people. We can see examples of this today; most recently, Trump called migrant refugees from Central America "animals," and since nonhumans are automatically seen as "less" than human, this form of speciesism is part of what helps society remove "value" from targeted groups. As history has shown us, when communities are devalued because they are seen as "less than," atrocities against them can be committed. For example, the Holocaust, slavery, the classification of First Nations Aboriginal people as wildlife, etc. Of course, in seeing nonhumans as less than humans, humans have been able to justify horrible atrocities against other species as well– and still do.

In an effort to bridge more gaps between social justice movements and communities like my own, I continued the conversation in my newest book *Veganism of Color: Decentering Whiteness in Human and Nonhuman Liberation.* The book attempts to open a dialogue between People of Color and Vegans of Color themselves, in an effort to reach our own communities in a way that validates them, but also helps them understand why veganism is important in our quest towards liberation for all– nonhumans and ourselves.

***Considering issues like that, such as white vegan activists invalidating the experiences of People of Color, how do you remain positive in your activism?***

At a certain point, I stopped focusing on the loudest voice in the room. I think it is easy to get caught up focusing on that one person instead of people who are on the fence and open to new ideas. As long as one person picks up my book and learns something from it, I think that's a win. That one person may be able to teach other people what they take from my work.

When I first released my board book, my work became public for the world to see, and I guess I experienced imposter syndrome. It helped to remember that what I'm doing is not about me. It's about who I can help, and that makes it all worth it.

Activism is about using the resources, knowledge, and passion that you have to create something that will help and contribute to all the other people that are also doing something. It doesn't have to be this huge thing that you're doing. It can be taking a supportive role or even donating your time or talents to a cause. Anything you can give to help is valuable. We can all make an impact where we are with what we have.

## Ruth Behar

Anthropologist

www.RuthBehar.com

—

"When we have gained the privilege of being heard, we have a duty to take action, beyond being passive observers to those in vulnerable situations."

*Ruth Behar is an influential anthropologist whose work is performed with a feminist consciousness. She is widely known for her early work that resulted in the book <u>Translated Woman: Crossing the Border with Esperanza's Story</u> (Beacon Press), as well as being the co-editor of a classic text on women's contributions to anthropology: <u>Women Writing Culture</u> (University of California Press). She combines ethnography, memoir, fiction, and poetry in her writing. Her other books include <u>The Vulnerable Observer: Anthropology That Breaks Your Heart</u> (Beacon Press) and <u>Traveling Heavy: A Memoir in between Journeys</u> (Duke University Press). One of the many contributions Ruth has made to her field is the discussion and validation of the "vulnerable observer," which allows for a compassionate and personal approach to anthropology. Most recently, she has written a middle-grade novel, <u>Lucky Broken Girl</u> (Puffin Books) that draws on her childhood experiences. Herein, Ruth discusses her journey to feminism, her work as an educator, and the important acts of storytelling and witnessing.*

—

My grandparents were immigrants to Cuba in the 1920s. They were from Poland and Russia on one side and Turkey on the other side. They were Jewish and were searching for a home at a time when economic, political, and emotional conditions were becoming very difficult in Europe. They found that home in Cuba. Therefore, my parents, my younger brother, and I were born there.

Havana, Cuba, is a beautiful place to be from, and we were part of a small but vibrant Jewish community in Havana. My family expected to always live there. Unfortunately, everything changed with the Cuban Revolution in 1959. My family, like many others, initially supported the revolution but then became disenchanted once the government did away with private enterprise. We left, along with thousands of Cubans, in the early 1960s, and came to the United States.

Unlike most Cubans, who settled in Miami, we settled in New York. I grew up in Queens, and, at the age of eighteen, I went off to college. I have visited New York often, and also Cuba, but never lived in either place again. I think of myself as being from Cuba *and* New York. I always thought I would go back to New York, just like I thought as a young woman that some time my family and I would go back and live in Cuba; but I never did.

I went to Wesleyan University as an undergraduate and Princeton as a graduate student. After college, I traveled for many years. After traveling to Spain and Mexico, I eventually found my way to Cuba in those years. However, I've now been living in Ann Arbor, Michigan for over thirty years. I've taught at the University of Michigan all of these years. I'm a very nomadic person, but, oddly enough, I created a lot of stability for myself by staying in Ann Arbor. I travel a lot, but I have a base that I always return to– my Midwest home, painted nine colors, including yellow, pink, blue, and green.

*I read in one of your interviews that you live with a suitcase by the door. Where do you think your love of traveling comes from? How has this shaped your life?*

I think my desire to travel, mainly to Spanish-speaking countries, comes from having been born in Cuba and having grown up with the Spanish language. When I was a child and a young woman, the Spanish language was a central force in my life. I think I wanted to "live in the language" as much as possible. I take great pleasure from speaking Spanish and hearing Spanish. There is something so exciting, effusive, and beautiful about the language. All of the different cadences, rhythms, and musicalities of Spanish move me deeply.

Spanish was the language of our emotions. It was the language of my family. For me, it was the language of lullabies and love. Of course, there are many Latinx in the United States, so you do not need to leave the country to speak Spanish with others, which is great; at the same time, there's definitely a tremendous electrical charge that I feel when I am immersed in the language in Spanish-speaking countries.

Travel is restorative, healing, and inspiring to me. There's something about being able to get from place to place in one piece that is marvelous. In my book, *Traveling Heavy*, I also write about how wonderful it is to be able to feel at peace with strangers. Even though for many, especially marginalized communities, the world can be dangerous, and our current political system has forced people from these communities to become more insular and cautious in their travels, my work as a cultural anthropologist has afforded me an experience in which I have been able to travel and have gotten to know the kindness of strangers. I have formed close and enduring friendships in Spain, Mexico, and my own native Cuba, all the countries where I have lived for extended periods of time. People have taken me into their homes and cooked meals for me. I feel a need to affirm these human bonds. It energizes me in hopeful ways and allows me to create bridges across ethnic, national, racial, class, and religious borders.

*That is beautiful. I have been fortunate to also experience the healing power of travel that you described. Now, when you look back on your life, can you see a path that led you to feminism, which is a big topic in your work?*

It is extremely clear how I became a feminist. I struggled with a very patriarchal, traditional, Cuban, Sephardic father. From the time I was a young girl, everything I wanted seemed wrong to him, including reading a lot of books and wanting to go off to college. I had to struggle to become an educated young girl and eventually, an educated woman. He thought a girl should wait at home until a man came to marry her. My father became upset when I applied to colleges against his will. Instead of congratulating me on receiving scholarships, he was furious. It was terrible; I was treated as an awful daughter who had disobeyed him.

When I was going through that period of wanting an

education, the feminist movement was underway. My struggles were more in the 1970s, but I was aware of the movement when I was a young girl in the 1960s. I was also aware of how my father treated my mother. He treated her as inferior. It was extremely painful to see. My father would say things to me like, "You're ruining your mother with your feminism." I was speaking up about gender inequality, and my mother was kind of going, "Yeah." He was thinking, "Wait a minute. I'm losing control now! Not just of my daughter, but my wife!"

We had these big struggles at home, but I still went off to college, very much against his will. Although I had a scholarship, it did not pay for all of my expenses, which made it difficult for me to stay in school. I chose to complete my undergraduate studies in three years by taking tutorials and summer courses because I was so concerned about the cost. I then went straight to graduate school at Princeton and studied anthropology, because they offered me a full scholarship and stipend. My education saved me. From an early age, I saw the importance of education for women to gain their freedom. Feminism and education go hand-in-hand.

### Did you notice any differences with the treatment of women versus men in your field?

Yes! I became very aware when I was a young assistant professor of how women in anthropology were treated differently from men. To this day, the people who are most revered as heroes are men doing these Indiana Jones kinds of projects, which are projects that would be very hard for a woman to do. We still have this gender imbalance, even in a field like anthropology that's supposed to be so self-aware and socially conscious. In the academic world, much work still needs to be done to value the work of women and to see that women have made, and continue to make, major contributions on the same level as men.

*In the preface to the most recent edition of __Translated Woman__, you state, "Ten years ago, I believed that, if every woman could tell her life story and be heard, we could change the world. I still believe it. I still believe it now." Can you speak to the power of storytelling and when it becomes a form of social justice?*

Stories are so important for all of us. We have seen, for example, in the MeToo movement, which was founded by civil rights activist Tarana Burke, that it all begins with a story. Tarana began the movement to raise awareness of sexual assault and abuse in society as a way to empower Women of Color through empathy and validation after a thirteen-year-old confided her own story of abuse to her one day. As we have seen through the thousands of stories from people that have come forth since then, a story can affect change. Stories articulate a truth and a reality. If you can tell a story that aches to be told, that has been silenced for too long, you can really start to change the world. You can create a social movement.

Storytelling is truly powerful when you have listeners. Stories need to be heard, and those of us that are in a place of privilege have a responsibility to listen. We've seen with MeToo how a lot of these stories existed long-ago and women had suffered from abuse and assault, but they hadn't been listened to, there wasn't yet a sympathetic audience to hear them because those living different experiences and untouched by these specific situations had not taken the time to listen. We reached a moment in our social, historical evolution where people began to listen, and in doing so, awareness was created, which led to the start of conversation and ultimately, change. So, storytelling and story-listening go together. It's a delicate dance between the two.

*I love the idea of listening and how important that is. This gets into the idea of what it means to be a witness. There are different ways you can be a witness and different actions you can take as a witness.*

That is very true. In my work as an observer, I am very concerned with this issue of witnessing and what happens when you witness horrible situations. In my life as an anthropologist, I've witnessed so many different things, including incredibly happy and beautiful moments, but also incredibly sad and tragic moments. I've heard so many terrible stories of suffering and loss. I've witnessed many people suffering from poverty and illness. To witness is to see, to observe, to be present; but what do you *do* with that? How do you actually reach out and help others?

In a way, it comes back to storytelling. Whether we are writers, anthropologists, or journalists, one of the ways we can be responsible is to tell a story that can lead listeners to open themselves to work towards justice and to see the humanity of others. When I read about the children being detained at the border, I'm so grateful to the journalists who are providing those stories for us. Those acts of witnessing are important. If it weren't for them, we wouldn't know how people are being mistreated and dehumanized. The journalists who pass on stories about such injustices are important witnesses and, in turn, become vulnerable observers. Our own role, however, can never stop with simply being witnesses. When we have gained the privilege of being heard, we have a duty to take action, beyond being passive observers to those in vulnerable situations.

*Your idea of the vulnerable observer and your book of the same title make me think about the pressure of not being too personal in the academic world—and, in a way, to deny our stories. One most basic example is not being able to write in the first person in academic writing.*

My undergraduate and graduate students are always surprised when I tell them I want them to write in the first person. They have been instructed to never use "I" and to maintain a distance between themselves and their work. The work is supposed to exist on its own and not have a connection to the person who is creating it. It has become clear to so many of us that it's just a very false way to work, because we are the filters through which we perceive reality. It's impossible not to be affected in some way. The personal is very much a part of whatever reality on which you're trying to shed light.

I tried my best to write in the classical academic way when I started out, but I was very unsatisfied with the results. I felt I left out too much. In fact, it was the inner, subjective part of my work that was important to share with others. I started to feel that the personal *had* to be inserted into academic work. It made the work more meaningful, as well as more insightful and interesting to the reader.

**Do you feel that you also try to be more personal as an educator in the classroom?**

Very much so. I teach a course on ethnographic writing, for example, and the students write about experiences that they themselves have had— either through field work, travel, or observing things at home. They're writing about experiences in which they themselves are in some way implicated. They end up sharing a lot of their life stories with their fellow students, and with me. This is not just in the writing, but in issues that come up for discussion in the classroom. I try to create a classroom that is a safe space where students can talk about complex emotional subjects very honestly.

I share personal stories with my students when they are relevant. Sometimes I'm asked to answer personal questions in the classroom, and I do share aspects of my life in our discussions. Things will also come up if we are talking about questions related to field work and I'll reminisce about my own experiences. I'll tell them about the challenges of being a young anthropologist in Spain in my early twenties, just after the death of Franco, and what that was like. I often tell stories about the relationships I formed through my field work and share personal experiences about my life in the academic world. It is not just me sharing, of course, because everyone in the class talks about the connections between their life and their work; so, during the semester, we become a very close community. I try to nurture bonds between the students, too. Instead of them just talking to me, I create a space in which everyone is talking to one another.

The classroom, for me, has become a really exciting space to not just share ideas or impart knowledge or pass along information...Those things happen, but it's also a very unique space for conversations that don't occur elsewhere, and for people to examine their vulnerability with one another. Students learn to share emotional experiences as well as intellectual ones. We talk about books, ideas, and writing; but we also talk about life.

**How do you see your work as a feminist anthropologist and educator as creating a better world for marginalized people?**

I entered the academy as a first-generation college-educated woman, and as a Latina, and I had to learn to navigate the complexities of the academy on my own. I bring that experience of doubt and anxiety, but also of determination and resilience, to my work as a feminist anthropologist and educator. I often work with students from marginalized sectors of our society who seek me out as a mentor because of my experience and my effort to serve as a bridge for these students, encouraging them to take risks and do the work that is meaningful to them and their communities.

As a scholar, I have tried to do research that sheds light on the struggles of marginalized people, and by sharing their stories, I hope that I raise awareness of how listening to those who have been rendered invisible, showing respect, and working together to bring their words to a larger public are an important step toward building a more egalitarian society. People who choose to tell their stories to a cultural anthropologist, like myself, often do so to validate experiences within their communities and to the wider world. When I recorded the story of Esperanza Hernández, a street peddler in Mexico, she always came accompanied by her younger son and daughter, so they could witness the importance I gave to her story. In the community, she had been labeled a "witch" because her abusive husband had gone blind after she left him. Esperanza wanted to prove to herself, to me, to her children, and to the world that she had been a victim of a violent patriarchal system; by listening to her story and writing a book about her (*Translated Woman: Crossing the Border with Esperanza's Story*), I could bring this truth to light.

We were both acutely aware of our differences; at the same time, we both believed that we had agency in our relationship. In fact, it was Esperanza who sought me out, convincing me that her story deserved to be in a book. As I wrote the book, drawing on the recorded interviews, I told her about everything that would appear in print and made sure to obtain her consent about every page before pursuing publication. Our work together was shared ethnography in the best sense of the term. Esperanza was so proud of the book that when it later came out in Spanish, at her request, she kept the book tucked away under her altar, where it would be safe and always available to her children and grandchildren. The book has also reached many readers beyond her family, as she hoped, who have sought to understand the complexity of working-class women's lives in Mexico and why it is important to make their stories known.

STACY RUSSO

## Steve Bell

Prison Library Project

www.ClaremontForum.org/Prison-Library-Project

—

"I want to help victims and people who are underrepresented."

*Steve Bell served nearly seventeen years of a life sentence in the California prison system for an attempted murder conviction. While in prison, he credits much of his rehabilitation and growth to access to books. Since his release, he has been a devoted activist through his work with the Prison Library Project, an organization that mails books to prisoners throughout the United States. While in prison, Steve became something of a "jailhouse lawyer." Upon his release, he received his law degree and passed the California Bar Exam on his first attempt. Although the California Bar has so far not admitted him due to his criminal conviction, he remains positive in pursuit of his dream: to practice law in California. Steve discusses his work with the Prison Library Project, as well as his additional activism related to elder abuse and a program he created: the Lifer Family Forum.*

—

I'm a native Californian, born in Culver City. I grew up in a fairly standard household for that day and age. My father worked and my mother kept the home. I was a Boy Scout, participated in marching band, and worked mowing lawns. I graduated from Charter Oak High School in Covina and went to Cal Poly Pomona. I received my bachelor's degree there and began an almost-twenty-year career in information technology.

In the early Nineties, I was living in northern California when I was arrested and convicted of attempted murder. I was sentenced to life with the possibility of parole, plus four years in California state prison. This was my first experience with the criminal justice system. Unlike most prisoners, lifers (a term I use to describe prisoners sentenced to indeterminate terms of life with the possibility of parole) must go before the parole board to determine if they are suitable for release. We have a board here in California called the Board of Parole Hearings, or BPH, made up of commissioners appointed by the governor. They hold parole hearings at different prisons around the state every week, at which they review lifers to determine if they are suitable for parole. The legal standard for suitability is whether the prisoner is currently an unreasonable risk of danger to society.

For many years, the parole board was sort of a political football. Under certain governors, the commissioners kept a lot of lifers inside a lot longer than the law had originally contemplated. Under Governor Pete Wilson, fewer than 100 lifers received parole. Gray Davis, even though he was a Democrat, was even worse; I think he only released two or three lifers during his entire term.

Today, there are almost 4,000 paroled lifers in California. They have the lowest recidivism rate of any class of prisoner. For the general population of prisoners released from prison, within three years, about 78% of them are back inside; for lifers, it is less than 1%. I believe it's because lifers have to earn their way out. When someone goes into prison with a determinant sentence, with a fixed number of years to serve, he can pretty much do whatever he wants. If you go in with a ten-year determinate sentence, you can refuse to work and even break the rules. It doesn't matter. When the ten years are up, you walk out. For these prisoners, there's no incentive in place to help rehabilitate them or to address the systemic root issues that got them there in the first place.

In contrast, lifers must earn their way out by proving that they have become rehabilitated. You have to demonstrate your rehabilitation in everything you do, every day, year after year. Once you've invested that amount of time in your own rehabilitation, chances are you won't screw up and go back to prison again. No former lifer in California has ever been convicted of a new life offense. When we get out, we tend to stay out, and we don't commit new serious offenses.

**Please tell me about your experience with libraries while in prison.**

While in prison, I fell into being a jailhouse lawyer by accident. Oddly enough, it all started with illiteracy. The level of illiteracy in our jails and prisons is astronomical. Prisoners as a whole read at about a third-grade level. Some have never been to school or held a job. My own estimate is that a large number of California prisoners are truly illiterate. I clearly remember one day early in my sentence when an old former gang "shot caller" came up to me holding a letter. A shot caller is someone who runs a prison gang, and who tells the gang members what to do. He had received a letter from his adult daughter, with whom he had been estranged for many years. He couldn't read the letter. Because of his status with his gang, he couldn't ask one of his homeboys to help him read it, so he came to me. He had seen that I spent lots of time writing letters and reading books. I read him his daughter's letter, and by the end of it, he had tears running down his face. His daughter was reaching out to him again, after all of these years of estrangement.

He asked me to read the letter to him again and then asked if I would help him write a response. I wrote word for word what he said, and he copied it in his own hand, letter by letter, and sent it to his daughter. They reconciled; it was very touching.

This sort of broke the ice for other prisoners. Somebody would come to me with a letter and say, "Can you read this to me?" Then somebody came to me with a letter from his attorney or a court document and asked, "Can you read this to me?" After I read it, their next question was, "Okay, what's it mean?" I had no clue; so, to find out, I started going to the prison's law library.

Almost any prisoner can go to the law library, but they don't tell you how anything works, how the books are organized, or where to find what you need. It took me years to figure it out, but I had a lot of time. I became good at finding where things were– the statutes, the court decisions, the legal procedures. I was able to start answering the questions.

For a while, I actually worked in the prison law library, and that helped a lot. Because it was my job assignment, I was in the library all day. At times, when the yard wasn't open, or when there were no prisoners there to help, I could do my own research. I started to learn more about how the law was organized. This also helped me fine-tune my research and writing skills.

*It sounds like access to the library's law resources was life-changing. What was your experience with books in general while in prison?*

In a larger sense, beyond the law library, books from the prison's recreational library and from sources outside of prison kept me sane. I usually read two or three books a week. I read all kinds of books, including novels, biographies, and whatever I could lay my hands on; I also read a lot of self-help books that helped me prepare for the parole board. I read hundreds of books when I was inside, and they helped my mind escape the walls.

Unfortunately, the recreational libraries are pretty much at the bottom of the totem pole when it comes to budget. They aren't open very often, and when they are, it's for very few hours, and the books get picked over pretty quickly. They also don't have the budget to replace them. Families can send books to prisoners, but the state of California currently only allows books from approved vendors, such as Amazon. There are also some organizations that do send you free books if you write and ask.

*How did you get involved with the Prison Library Project?*

After I came home, I was in Claremont, California, looking for a 50th wedding anniversary gift for my aunt and uncle, when I saw a sign that said, "Prison Library Project Bookstore." I had only been out for a few months. I walked in and discovered it was a beautifully-appointed used bookstore. It turned out that one of the board members was sitting at the table where they normally have a cashier.

I got to talking with the board member, and she told me about the project, which has been sending free books to prisoners since the mid-1980s. By the time she was done talking to me, I had teared up; it was perfect. This was something that I could do to help others who were going through what I went through in prison. I started volunteering there. We get requests in the mail from prisoners nationwide and try to fulfill them as best as we can. Letters requesting books arrive daily. We have tens of thousands of books in our inventory, and more are donated all of the time. We send out about 30,000 free books to prisoners every year.

Because of the demand, we ask each prisoner to request books only every six months. We try to keep all of the mailings to two pounds or less, because that way we can service more prisoners with our limited budget. The problem with a lot of the educational books, like the GED workbooks, is that they weigh four and five pounds each. Occasionally, we bite the bullet budget-wise and send out some larger books if, in reading the letter, we feel that the situation is exceptional.

Some of the budget to run the project comes from purchases at the bookstore, some from donations, and some from fundraising events throughout the year. The parent organization for the Prison Library Project is the Claremont Forum. The Claremont Forum sponsors a weekly organic farmer and artisans' market, and proceeds from this also help fund the Prison Library Project.

I think the recidivism rate would be less if prisoners engaged more with books while they were inside; this could be books beyond educational and self-help— books that broaden someone's horizon and get them to engage with the world in a different way. I believe whole-heartedly in the positive role played by the Prison Library Project in supplying free books to prisoners. I started as a volunteer almost seven years ago, and I joined the board two years ago. Last month, I was elected president of the board.

However, the high illiteracy rate is a root issue that also needs to be addressed systematically, in addition to providing access to books. Addressing illiteracy would not only help prisoners when they return to society, but it would also help them feel like they're a part of our wider society *while* in prison and working towards something better for themselves.

**What other types of activism and community work have you been involved with, beyond the Prison Library Project?**

I have used my education and experience to help in other ways, including work with the Elder Abuse Restraining Order Clinic. It is a joint project between the Legal Aid Society of Orange County and the Orange County Superior Court. The clinic helps elders and dependent adults fill out and file the paperwork needed to get them before a judge to get restraining orders against abusers.

My interest in elder law might be seen as somewhat

self-serving, I guess, since I'm within a couple of years of being, legally, an elder. However, part of me just really dislikes the whole concept of abuse of those who are who are weaker, smaller, or older by bigger, stronger, or younger people. I volunteer at the clinic every Tuesday. Sadly, there are far too many elders in need of restraining orders. Family members and caregivers seem to be the biggest culprits when it comes to elder abuse. A lot of it is pretty sad, and it makes me mad enough to do a good job. Give me an elder that's been abused, and I'll go to the mat to help them.

Another project that is very near and dear to my heart is one I created, called the Lifer Family Forum. It's a series of workshops for people in the community who have loved ones who are serving life sentences in California prisons. We have upwards of 30,000 men and women in California prisons serving indeterminate life sentences. All of them will have to go before the parole board and prove that they are not an unreasonable risk of danger to society.

When I was inside, my family felt helpless and didn't know how the lifer parole system worked, what to do, or how to help me to come home. I remember how badly I felt about this, and, because I didn't really know how the system worked, either, I couldn't help them. We eventually figured it out, and I eventually came home; but I remember the pain, frustration, and hopelessness. I started this project so that other families will have some kind of hope.

In these seminars, I give families the nuts and bolts of how the parole system works and how they can help their lifer prepare for the parole board. I am very careful to explain right up front that, since I am not an attorney, I cannot give them legal advice, but only general legal information. I am really careful about this, because I don't want the State Bar to misperceive that I'm practicing law without a license. I'm reapplying to the Bar in August, and I want them to admit me this time. I cover the need for lifers to gain insight into their crimes and the actions and attitudes underlying those crimes. I describe the importance of developing remorse for their crimes and all of the harm it caused not just to the victims, but also to their families and the community at large. There is a concept that when someone commits an act of violence, it's like throwing a stone into a pond: the harm keeps rippling outwards from the crime itself through everyone touched by it and society as a whole.

I discuss the concepts of making amends, of having a relapse prevention plan and a realistic parole plan, and of developing a network in the community to support lifers when they are released. Ultimately, I help them understand what the process is and how they can help their lifer get through that process. I'm trying to help other families not go through what my family went through; I do this work four times a year at my own expense, and I don't charge anyone for it. I have a little donation jar in the back, and, if somebody wants to drop some money in, that'll help.

I do a similar kind of thing where I take the same information and change the focus, then go back into prisons and give classes to the lifers themselves. I recently finished one at C.I.M., the women's prison in Chino. It was a fifteen-week, one-night-a-week class that went through parole hearing preparation in great detail. I had about eighty lifers in the room.

**What do you desire to do as a future practicing attorney? How will your work contribute to creating a better world for marginalized people?**

There are so many populations who are underserved by lawyers and the legal system. Lifers are one example. Elder abuse victims are another example. I hope that eventually, the State Bar will admit me as an attorney, because there are so many people who need legal assistance.

I believe that taking a case simply for a paycheck is wrong. I think you should take a case that you believe in, and that's how I want to practice law. I admit that I have a real David and Goliath complex. I want to represent the Davids against the Goliaths of the world.

I knew before I went to law school that my conviction would pose certain barriers, and I'm doing all that I can to overcome them. I remain hopeful that the Bar will admit me. It's ironic that, at a time when my high school and college friends are retiring, I'm working so hard to start a whole new career.

**Kamekə Brown**

Farm Sanctuary

www.FarmSanctuary.org

—

"Arriving at Farm Sanctuary was a healing experience."

*Kamekə Brown's life is an example of the awakening, dedication, and evolution of an activist's journey from a young age. After graduating with a bachelor's degree from the University of Texas in Austin, she served three terms in AmeriCorps. This experience provided her with a diverse array of activism experience related to social justice and environmental action. After discovering veganism, Kamekə interned at Farm Sanctuary and ultimately became a volunteer Program Coordinator. At the time of this interview, she is preparing to begin a new role with the organization as a Humane Educator for Los Angeles schools. Here, Kamekə talks about her earlier service work with AmeriCorps, her journey coming out as a Queer Black Womxn, how veganism became part of her daily life, the meaning of sanctuary for farm animals and all oppressed beings, and her family of two adopted dogs.*

—

When I think about my early life, I feel this strong inclination to give background and context regarding my family. I feel like knowing my parents' background and the background of my ancestors is necessary in order to fully understand who *I* am. My mom and her side of the family were immigrants from Trinidad and Tobago. They came to the United States when she was around thirteen or fourteen years old. She, her siblings, and her parents moved to New York City. My dad's parents were people of African descent whose families had been living in the United States for generations. My dad was born and raised in New York City.

My parents met in the military. While my dad attended college, he attempted to figure out the most secure future for himself; to him, the military seemed to be the best option. My mom was in college and became pregnant with my older brother during her studies. After giving birth, she felt that the best way for her to care for my brother was to join the military as well.

My parents got married and had my middle brother and I while still in the military. During this time, we moved around a lot. I was born in Fairbanks, Alaska; six months to a year after I was born, we moved to Texas. We moved about every three years– mostly to different towns in Texas. When I was in the third or fourth grade, we moved to Germany.

We lived in Wiesbaden, Germany for a few years. At that time, my oldest brother, Nathaniel– we call him Natty– was an adult and living on his own. So, it was only my parents, my middle brother, and I who lived abroad. Living in Germany was a really great experience for my family, as we were part of a very close-knit community of families with other children who were also living on the military base. I believe we developed this close-bonded community around our shared experience as military kids living abroad because we felt isolated.

My family and I traveled around Europe and visited some of my mom's relatives from Trinidad who had migrated there. It was such a beautiful time that I definitely look back on it as one of my favorite moments from my childhood.

After we left Germany, we moved to Montgomery, Alabama, which was a bit of a shock and a difficult adjustment for my brother and I. In Germany and at the military base, we were surrounded by a really diverse group of kids from different backgrounds who had connected with one another and built a community. Montgomery, Alabama was the first time that I really came face- to-face with racism and the history of segregation in the Deep South. It was so different from the experience I'd had in Germany. In Alabama, I was forced to grapple with what it meant for me to be a young Black girl in a world that I was beginning to think hated me. It deeply impacted how I saw myself and how I navigated and showed up in the world.

I didn't realize it then, but it was the beginning of a transformative journey of self-exploration and identity for me. Up until that point, I'd had a certain level of comfort and security within my family and the community I had in Germany. However, moving to Alabama made me aware of the world beyond my family and the places where I felt safe. Most profoundly, I realized that the world felt a certain way about me simply because I was a Black girl, and I was overwhelmed by how out-of-my-control it felt. Even still, that experience of community that I'd had in Germany stuck with me.

*That's powerful. It must have been difficult to reconcile these realizations with the experiences of a community you once had. What happened next?*

In high school, I developed an appreciation for Marie Curie and what I was reading about her life. I came across a quote in which she says, "You cannot hope to build a better world without first improving the individuals. To that end, each of us must work for [our] own improvement and, at the same time, share a general responsibility for all humanity. Our particular duty being to aid those to whom we think we can be most useful."

At the time I discovered the quote, I was trying to imagine my life beyond high school and kind of saw that quote as a road map; it grounded me in wanting to figure out how I could help the world and make a difference. I went to college at the University of Texas in Austin and double-majored in psychology and Plan II honors, which is an interdisciplinary liberal arts honors degree. My college experience was a continuation of my journey towards understanding myself and the world.

As a college student, I studied abroad in Ghana for a month. This was a really powerful experience for me. It gave me a different kind of understanding of myself and my ancestors and gave me a perspective of a world beyond one that centered whiteness. That experience abroad and what I was learning in psychology and the other courses I was taking were all really formative in shaping my worldview. Originally, my plan had been to go to graduate school for psychology after finishing college; but my experience in Ghana had inspired me to want to be in community, be of service, and see more of the world. I had also seen Barack Obama speak in Austin when he was running for president, and he spoke about how being involved in community organizing was a critical part of his journey. Having that kind of experience of community and service felt like it would be important for me. So, right after I finished college, I applied to AmeriCorps National Civilian Communion Corps (NCCC), a team-based national service program.

That summer, while I was waiting to hear back about my application, I did another AmeriCorps program, VISTA or Volunteers in Service to America. I worked as a summer youth counselor at Wesley-Rankin Community Center in Dallas, working directly with youth to support them in navigating the transition from adolescence to adulthood.

In the Fall, I started my first term of service with AmeriCorps NCCC out of Sacramento, California, where I worked on a variety of projects with a team of other young adults. Our first project was focused on environmental stewardship in San Francisco at the Presidio and involved tasks like setting up garden beds and invasive species removal. Another project we did was in Hawaii, at a place called Camp Mokule'ia in Oahu. This project was focused on helping the camp become more sustainable through the construction of recycling and rainwater catchment systems. While there, we also helped build a greenhouse and expand their garden.

Other work that I took part in included a project in the Mendocino National Forest, where we did trail building; and, later, a fire mitigation project at Camp Sacramento, near Lake Tahoe. My team also worked with an organization called Loaves and Fishes in Sacramento that provides resources for those experiencing homelessness. That was one of my favorite projects because of the incredible people—mostly children—with whom I connected.

AmeriCorps was definitely a key formative experience for me. Although I had planned to attend graduate school after finishing the program, my time with AmeriCorps helped me to realize that there are so many different possibilities for what we can do in the world. My experiences of community, travel, and direct service had deeply inspired me.

While I was in AmeriCorps, I had also fallen in love with another woman in the program and began to grapple with understanding myself as a Queer person. I came out to my family right after finishing AmeriCorps, and it wasn't exactly well-received. My relationship with that woman ended, and I moved to New Jersey and started graduate school. It was like a storm of so many things during a very difficult time of transition in my life, and I struggled to handle and navigate it all.

*What was your experience in graduate school?*

I was accepted into a psychology doctoral program at Rutgers University. While in the program, I did individual and group therapy with clients and, admittedly, felt a lot of frustration with that work. It seemed I was coming to them too late, after they had already experienced major difficulty and trauma, and I became curious about how to intervene *before* it got to that point. I wondered how we could make changes on a systemic level, rather than trying to patch-up the individual— as if *they* were the problem! I was still trying to make sense of myself and the world, and where I fit in and could best help. I left after a year and a half. It was a difficult experience, but it was a liberating one to know that I could always make the choice to leave when something is not working. I didn't need to feel obligated to follow the path that I once thought I should have followed, or that society or anyone else tells me I should follow. At this point, I was still trying to figure out what it meant to navigate the world as a Queer Black Womxn. It was overwhelming! I felt this push to do something and counteract the helplessness I felt. I was still committed to the words of the Marie Curie quote and wanted to know what I had to offer and contribute to the world. It was around that time that I first began to learn about veganism.

**Please tell me more about your discovery of veganism and how this has played a role in your activism work.**

I began to learn about the treatment of farmed animals in our society, and to understand that I had been complicit in the harm they experience. Learning about veganism was an epiphany-moment in which I realized that my complicity wasn't out of necessity— that there was a different choice I could make. I connected with a friend who had gone vegan and, after speaking with them about it, I spent that weekend delving into all things related to veganism and the treatment of farmed animals. I learned so much about the consequences of our use and treatment of farmed animals, which does not affect only them, but also humans and our planet. I realized that our treatment of farmed animals was consistent with my understanding of injustice and oppression. A vegan lifestyle felt like a tangible thing that I could adopt that was at the intersection of so many of the issues about which I cared deeply. I realized it was an extension of my commitment to being counter-oppressive, and that it was a way for me to live that commitment daily. It was in alignment with how I wanted to live my life and what I value. This was a profound shift for me.

### How did you find your way to Farm Sanctuary?

My journey to Farm Sanctuary was kind of a continuation of my work with AmeriCorps. I did a second term of service with AmeriCorps as a team leader and, when that program ended, I wanted to do work that was directly related to farmed animals. What I had learned about veganism had become important to my understanding of anti-oppression work and creating a better world. I wanted to engage in similar direct service and action to better the world in a way that was explicitly related to farmed animals, especially considering my complicity in the harm they experience. I applied to intern with Farm Sanctuary and was accepted at its Northern California shelter in Orland, California.

It was a really significant experience because, although I had made the transition to living a vegan lifestyle, I did not personally know or have relationships with any farmed animals. At Farm Sanctuary, I was actually able to be in community with them and to get to know them as individuals. This brought a whole new level of meaning and depth to my veganism. I understood the importance of the work in a different way, who the individuals behind the issue were; I was introduced to the concepts of sanctuary and multi-species community.

Sanctuaries are often situated in rural communities surrounded by animal farms, so it was really powerful for these spaces to exist as a sort-of oasis from that larger community. When you drive to the sanctuary, you pass all of these farms where the animals are destined to lives of oppression, use, and exploitation; then, you arrive at the sanctuary, and it's a radically different space and environment. It's a space that seeks to counter the normalization of animal use and oppression. It prioritizes non-human animals' individual care, wants, and desires.

It also gave me a vision for myself, particularly as a Queer Black Womxn, of the power and possibility of creating radically liberating spaces in an oppressive world—that we need not wait to actualize that reality. Arriving at Farm Sanctuary was a healing experience. I fell in love with the potential of that space and the power of sanctuary. I applied for a staff position as Volunteer Program Coordinator at its New York shelter, and was hired. It felt important for me to create meaningful opportunities for service and to empower others in their ability to contribute to transformative work and make a difference.

### Are you still the volunteer program coordinator?

No, I'm actually transitioning into a new role with Farm Sanctuary— a Humane Educator. I will be going into schools in the Los Angeles area and giving presentations about Farm Sanctuary and our food system in the United States. The presentation explores the impact of our food system on farmed animals, workers, communities, and the environment.

**You now also have a two-dog family. What has your experience with dog adoption been like?**

After I moved to New York to work with Farm Sanctuary, I adopted a dog from a rescue. They were having trouble placing him, so he was going to be euthanized—in part because he is a black dog who resembles a pit bull. So, I took him in, and our journey together has been a learning experience for both of us. I love him *so* much. It was overwhelming at first, but I was committed to him as a partner. His name is Chaz.

We're learning so much together—how to communicate with one another and navigate the world. I try to teach him what he needs to know to be safe in a human world and constantly grapple with balancing his own agency as an individual with teaching him things that are necessary for his survival. It's been a challenge—especially because society has certain perceptions of dogs who look and act like him. However, I wouldn't trade this experience for anything; he's my partner. We recently also took in a Chihuahua puppy named Kaia, so now, it's the three of us. This is my family, and there's so much love between Chaz and Kaia.

My partnerships with Chaz and Kaia have further broadened my understanding of the beauty, power, and importance of multi-species community. Those of us who share our homes with cats, dogs, rabbits, hamsters, etc. are already living in intentional multi-species community—communities of care and respect, in which we must thoughtfully navigate what it means to be in relationship with one another. Farmed animal sanctuaries like Farm Sanctuary present one model of multi-species community on a large scale, but there are micro-models of multi-species community with farmed animals, as well—for example, families who share their homes with chickens in urban or more suburban settings. I think it can be really powerful to expand and explore our notions of community and relationship with other species. There are so many animals, farmed animals especially, in need of homes where they are given the freedom they deserve and the appropriate care necessary for their well-being, survival, and thriving. Whether by supporting larger farmed animal sanctuaries or cultivating micro-sanctuaries in our own homes, I truly believe that one of our most accessible doorways to a better world is through the communities we create.

***It's wonderful to share about multi-species families like yours.***

***As you work to continue to create community and better the world, how do you stay encouraged in your activism?***

My experience of sanctuary has given me so much hope about what's possible. It keeps me rooted in the beauty and power of what we have the ability to create. It's inspired me to continuously inquire into what it looks like to cultivate spaces and relationships that offer hope, love, and healing and that embody what it means to be counter-oppressive.

There's so much in the world that feels like it's beyond our control, but sanctuary and veganism and my work and my experiences have really taught me what we each have the power to create. I have witnessed our ability to make a difference in so many ways. In my personal life, I've realized that I have so much power to engage in practices that promote healing and counter oppression. I know that I can engage in my relationships in ways that reflect that desire and that commitment and the communities I've shared in and been a part of affirm that hope and possibility. They keep me grounded in my—and our– ability and power to create a better world, even when imaging a different world might seem impossible. That's what keeps me hopeful and determined.

# Judy Grahn

Poet

www.JudyGrahn.org / www.CommonalityInstitute.org

—

"I keep learning from poetry."

*Judy Grahn is an activist, poet, and scholar. In 1965, she picketed at the White House for gay rights with East Coast Homophile Organizations. Then, in 1969, she founded the Women's Press Collective and Gay Women's Liberation, both of which supported the women's movement of the 1970s and 1980s through projects including education centers/bookstores, presses, health centers, and battered women's shelters. Judy's poetry celebrates queer identity, feminism, working-class life, and her personal experiences as a lesbian. She is truly a people's poet through her subjects and use of plain language, making her poems highly accessible to a wide audience. She is also notable for her veneration of everyday people and experiences. This is beautifully demonstrated in her influential early collection titled <u>The Work of a Common Woman</u> (Diana Press). Judy is also a scholar of Metaformic Consciousness, which she presents in the book <u>Blood, Bread, and Roses: How Menstruation Created the World</u> (Beacon Press). Her other works include her memoir <u>A Simple Revolution: The Making of an Activist Poet</u> (Aunt Lute), <u>Another Mother Tongue: Gay Words, Gay Worlds</u> (Beacon Press), <u>The Judy Grahn Reader</u> (Aunt Lute), and the poetry collections <u>Love Belongs to Those Who Do the Feeling</u> (Red Hen Press) and <u>Hanging on Our Own Bones</u> (Arktoi Books). Judy has been the recipient of over twenty awards, including several Lambda Literary Awards and a National Endowment for the Arts individual grant for poetry.*

—

I was born in Chicago in 1940. I lived there with my parents and an older brother and sister who left home by the
time I was six or eight. My father worked in a factory in
Chicago, but it was way too harsh of a working environment. Because of this, he moved us out to New Mexico
when I was eight years old. Even though my parents
dropped out of high school in the ninth grade and really
struggled to hold a material life together, they were fasci-
nating in many other ways, and gave me what I needed in
my life to be a poet.

I came out to myself at the age of fifteen or sixteen. I
understood that I was a lesbian and that I was different
from other people. I didn't know anyone else who was
like me. In that day and age, no one was talking about
sexuality. I was struggling to find out who I was; I was
also literally starving to death in New Mexico, trying to
earn a living as a single woman working in a restaurant.
As is true for so many people today, I could put a roof
over my head, but I could not afford food, heat, or elec-
tricity. To find a way to support myself, I joined the Air
Force; but it kicked me out for being a lesbian. That was a
very radicalizing moment for me, and it sort of set the
course of my life— that, coupled with the fact that I'm a
poet, and have been a poet since age nine.

**When I was reading your memoir, it was interesting
to me how life for you as a young girl in New Mexico
was so different from your earlier life in Chicago.
Can you tell me about this experience?**

Chicago in the 1940s was a harsh environment for working-class people. I think my whole family felt this way. One example I can think of is where we lived. It was a one-bedroom apartment, and there was a tiny patch of grass outside. However, the children were not allowed to play on it. We played war games in the alley, on the cement bunkers that held the trash cans. There was always an aura of violence and threat that surrounded us.

New Mexico was different. Where we lived in New Mexico was an absolutely gorgeous part of the country, with mountains and diverse forms of nature. There were all kinds of birds and reptiles. I remember a horned toad that I encountered the first day we were there. I was ecstatic to hold that creature in my hand. It was just *amazing!* The little brown toad had horns all over it, with eyes looking at me. That was incredible. There was so much life and beauty. It had a spiritual nature to it that was very appealing to me.

The town in New Mexico also had a softer social context that made things easier for my parents; it was definitely a much better environment for us all— especially my mother, who struggled with her mental health.

*I want to ask you about something that happened when you were fifteen in New Mexico that you mention in **A Simple Revolution**. You went to see a live performance of **A Midsummer Night's Dream** and you saw the character Puck. That seemed like a very significant experience.*

When I was fifteen, I had outgrown the label "tomboy." There were no words for the kind of person that I am. I have a low voice. I wear gender-neutral clothing. I knew that I was not only a lesbian, but some kind of gender non-binary person. There was no language for that then. The word "non-binary" was not in the vocabulary. There were slang words in the gay underground, which I hadn't yet discovered, such as *gay* and *dyke*. The kids at school knew the word *queer*, but I just thought that meant someone who was different.

In *A Midsummer Night's Dream*, Puck is the kind of person who's a little outside of the action but provides an overview about what is happening with the different characters. Puck is not one of the heterosexual characters. Puck is outside of that. Puck is a "fairy" person. Puck is this very gender non-binary character who is beautiful but read as a boy. Or, not exactly a boy, but possibly a man who could be played by a woman. Puck represents beauty and strength, and someone who is a little outside of the rest of society. That's what caught my attention. I saw myself reflected for the first time. I said, "That's who I am."

*That is a beautiful story and shows the power of art and what art can do for somebody.*

*With regards to your life as a poet, I've recommended your __Common Woman Poems__ to so many students and other people over the years since I discovered them as a young woman. What led to the creation of these poems from your early life and perhaps experiences in consciousness-raising groups? Were you surprised by the impact?*

In the 1960s, consciousness-raising groups were extremely valuable to women who were seeking changes in their lives for all kinds of reasons, since they provided women a place in which to discuss their personal experiences. I was invited to one, but I found myself really uncomfortable, and I never went back. The people there were talking about their lives, and I burst out with a notification that I was a lesbian. Some women in the group were frightened of lesbians. I was so sensitive about this because I had never seen myself reflected, aside from the Puck character.

Nothing in the arts or the public sphere was reflecting who I was. I didn't realize that was true for millions of women, not just lesbian women or dyke women. Millions of women had not seen themselves reflected in the culture at all. I came to write the poems in *Common Woman Poems* out of feeling hurt and tired of being left out. I wrote the poems as a kind of exercise for myself; at the same time, it was my own fictionalized consciousness-raising group that I was sort of inventing in the poems themselves. Each poem was either based on a person I knew or based on a composite of several people. I drew from my knowledge about other people I had known, including people I had known in Washington, D.C. when I lived there. There was a Black woman who was sort of the mother of my D.C. neighborhood. She took care of six or eight kids who were not hers. This kind of act is overlooked as a way of holding communities— and, ultimately, society— together. I wanted to bring awareness to examples like that in those poems, and I think they came pretty close to doing that.

I tied together all of these very different real-life women, who I fictionalized in my prose with this end line of each poem: "The common woman is as common as..." and included a noun or descriptor. For example, I used words like a thunderstorm, a crow, a nail, or the best of bread that will rise. I wrote them all in one night, while listening to Nina Simone sing a Leonard Cohen song about a woman who was mysterious.

At the time, there was such an absence of women and other marginalized people seeing themselves reflected in the arts while, historically, the common man has been represented. Van Gogh, for example, got in trouble with the Church because he was painting ordinary people. In the 1920s and 1930s, we saw common men represented during the labor movement, but working-class women had not seen themselves reflected. When I wrote the poems in 1969, women were learning how to empathize with themselves and with other women. It was amazing how many people just gravitated to the poems and ran with them, and they are still doing that because to see yourself reflected is incredibly important. Out of this grew my concept of commonality to locate similarities in the midst of differences. In fact, this eventually led to the formation of the Commonality Institute by two younger people, Anya de Marie and Gregory Gajus, with a focus of studying my work.

*That is wonderful to hear about the forming of the institute. Let me ask you about another major part of your work, which is Metaformic Consciousness. If someone was not familiar with this, how would you describe it?*

Metaformic Consciousness is a new, inclusive origin story of human evolution based on rituals— especially blood rituals, including peaceful ones surrounding menstruation.

These were once very elaborate rituals; they functioned as forms of school. Even though these rituals have largely been replaced by other forms of education, it is still possible to learn from old accounts of them and to see roots of human culture and women's places in culture through them.

Metaformic Consciousness does not displace men; instead, it repositions women and other genders. It helps with cross-cultural understanding and also helps us realize how we differ and don't from other creatures.

I had an interest in science and thought that, if I explored menstruation history, then I would come upon some contributions that women had made to culture with regard to calendars and time, including things like lunar timing and farming calendars. This included how farmers would plant at night by the moon or during certain seasons. I researched this for over twenty years. Then, in 1984, I published an article about it. By the time I wrote my book *Blood, Bread, and Roses: How Menstruation Created the World*, I had developed a theory around women's contributions to culture following my theory that we are ritual beings, and our ancestors performed rituals around menstruation and the womb. Ultimately, Metaformic Consciousness gives us a lot of clues about how to go about making changes in ourselves, society, and in relationships.

I taught Metaformic Consciousness as the primary theory in a women's spirituality master's program that I co-directed for thirteen or fourteen years. The theory will be a part of what the Commonality Institute is teaching.

*In __A Simple Revolution__, you discuss the importance of honesty and authenticity for poets and writers. You state, "Even at this young age, I knew myself as a writer and that writing is about justice." You also mention truth-telling within this context. Can you share your thoughts on this?*

It is important to take the power of art seriously. There is always something in poetry that is about honesty. In some ways, it arouses empathy for oneself and for others. I try to impart to my students to take themselves and their art seriously. Once you know how to do something and you develop the skills, then the question is, "Why are you doing it?" In the case of poetry, it's like a spiritual calling. You're not doing it for the money or for anything that's really self-aggrandizing, because it's difficult to write poetry.

Poetry is powerful. It is at the forefront of activism because people are fed by it. If you are a community poet like I am, then your ear is always to the ground about people's concerns. You ask, "How can poetry teach something?" It's inherent in art that the artist doesn't know the answer when they start creating. You don't know where it's going to go. You can think you know and can aim your work in some direction, but you are going to learn along the way. I keep learning from poetry.

Decades later, I can go back and read mine or someone else's poetry and still learn something new. It's almost like a form of divination, but it's also about being a reporter on behalf of truth. That is what it's like for me.

*You also mention in your memoir that being a poet*

*is a gift and a responsibility, but you further state that there is a danger to it. I imagine the danger aspect could be tied into activism and truth-telling.*

Yes, I think that's right. As a whole, woman writers have been telling the truth on behalf of women for the last forty or fifty years. Truth-telling poetry triggers all kinds of reactions and opens the doors of possibilities. It's a way of seeing and communicating what has been overlooked and needs to be changed or revealed. Truth-telling poetry also challenges the power structure. There's always a danger involved in that.

For me, poetry is a kind of prophecy, since the poem knows more than I do, which is one reason I write. For instance, if I have a question about something, then my poetry will address the question, and, in the process, I will think, "Oh, I didn't know it was going to go in that direction." To a great extent, my poetry has been part of the social movements that I've been involved with, as well as my own lived experiences. I've had a really interesting life. It has taken many twists, turns, ups, and downs. Through this, poetry has constantly taught me something that I didn't know before. I find that to be extraordinary.

*Overall when you consider your long career and what is still to come in the future, how do you see your work as contributing to the creation of a better world for marginalized people?*

I write from the base of community. My work has influenced the LGBT and Queer, Feminist, and Women's Spirituality movements. I have used my poetry and prose to create new origin stories and power metaphors that help move groups and individuals who had been marginalized into more central positions.

I am hopeful that the Commonality Institute will contribute to making the world better through an exploration and study of commonality to see how we are uniquely different and how we can cherish and respect those differences. Commonality starts from standing in your own being and looking across at others standing where they are in their beings and noticing what overlaps and what can be in common between us.

## Bamby Salcedo

TransLatin@ Coalition

www.TransLatinaCoalition.org

—

"The message was that we can do whatever we want with our bodies without society dictating what we can and cannot do."

*Bamby Salcedo is the founder of TransLatin@ Coalition, a Los Angeles-based organization with a mission "to organize and advocate for the needs of Trans Latin@s who are immigrants and reside in the US." After many years of personal struggle and experiencing great trauma, Bamby sought help and transformed her life. She is an inspiration and light for all who suffer from great oppression. Here she shares her story, including the tragedies she experienced at the hands of law enforcement as a transgender woman, how she overcame, and, ultimately, what led her to create TransLatin@ Coalition and become an amazing and passionate advocate for her community.*

—

CW: sexual abuse, violence, drug use

I was born on October 12, 1969, in Guadalajara, Jalisco, Mexico, to a single mother. My father left my mother before I was born. My mother was a very hard-working woman who wanted the best for us. Since she was young, she didn't really know how to provide other than being able to work. She eventually got together with another man, who became my stepfather. When I was three years old, I started being sexually abused by this individual. I was searching for love and thought there may be a way for this person to love me. I did what I needed to do. My mother didn't really know that anything was happening.

Early in my childhood, I knew who I was. I already had a sense of my gender identity. However, because I was assigned male at birth and was the oldest in my family, there were a lot of social and cultural expectations put on me that conflicted with my identity. When I was about eight years old, I started using drugs. I was simply a troubled child who was seeking love. I was miserable and trying to find myself. I tended to find myself through the pain.

**Thank you for sharing that difficult part of your early story. When did you come to the United States?**

I was first institutionalized in Mexico when I was twelve years old. I kept getting into trouble and was arrested. I was put in juvenile halls and other places. I started to come out around this age, too. I was hanging out with members of the LGBTQ community in Guadalajara, since I could be my true self with them. I was literally betraying the expectations of the life of a boy. Because my mother didn't really know how to take care of me or how to deal with everything that was going on, she suggested I should come to the United States and live with my father.

I was seventeen when I came here. I didn't really know my father or anything about him. Obviously, I wanted him to love me and accept me for who I was. When I came to the United States, like so many undocumented people, I was exploited as a minor. I worked in a tortilla factory for the first two years. I didn't speak any English or know anything about this country.

When I was living in Los Angeles around age nineteen, I decided it was time for me to start my transition. At that time, obviously, there wasn't any support. I would only find support on the streets, from other transwomen. This was a difficult time. I had no stable housing, so I was homeless. I also used drugs and found myself going to jail in Los Angeles. I spent about fourteen years of my life going in and out of jail. I was also deported four different times.

My experiences with law enforcement in Mexico involved being sexually abused by the police. I was beat up. One time they picked me up, and they shaved my head and sexually assaulted me before beating me up and leaving me on the outskirts of the city.

The last time I got out of prison in Mexico, I came back to Los Angeles. All I knew was how to function in the street economy with drugs, sex work, and stealing. My life was nothing at the time, but I wanted to do something different because otherwise, I knew I would die, somebody would kill me, or I would end up in prison for a long time. I had had guns pointed to my head. I attempted suicide multiple times. I had been dragged from cars. I had overdosed and been left for dead; but, somehow, I'm still here. Through divine intervention, I found a way to get my life together again.

*I find it remarkable that, in the midst of all the trauma you experienced, you were able to pull yourself out and build a new life. When you said it was due to "divine intervention," can you tell me more about that?*

While being homeless, using drugs, and doing all you do when you're on the streets, I remember a moment where I felt my life and my soul were shattered. I was unhappy and experiencing so much pain and sadness. I asked God to help me.

I was in Downtown Los Angeles on this one particular night, after having smoked crack for thirty days, when I reached out to God. I was hungry and miserable. The next day, I asked someone for money. It was a gay woman. She gave me five dollars and something to eat. I ended up getting on a bus. I fell asleep and somehow, when I finally got off of the bus, I found that I was at a treatment center. My request was answered, and suddenly, my new life began.

I went into the treatment center and asked to be admitted. They told me to come back the next day. I said that if I left, I knew I was not going to come back and something horrible was going to happen. They saw my desperation and admitted me. I always say that I'm a miracle.

I was thirty-one at the time, and I was determined to attain a better life. I started organizing and getting involved in social justice. There were people who were part of the LGBTQIA+ community in the treatment center, and they had started a support group that I joined.

## Do you feel that's when you started to become an activist?

Yes, in some ways, you could say that. Besides organizing, I motivated people when I spoke to them. I got some seniority after being there for a few months, so I was able to ask people to participate in the support group. At that point, my career of advocacy and organizing had begun.

## What happened with your activism work over the next few years?

To graduate from the treatment center, you had to be working or be in school. Because I was undocumented and had been deported multiple times, I was not able to work. Also, at the time, it was difficult for a transwoman to get a job. Because of this, I enrolled in adult school. I didn't know anything about computers— not even how to turn one on! I started attending a basic computer class. I learned how to type, how to navigate the Internet, how to open a Word document, and how to type a letter.

When I got out of the treatment center, I went into a transitional housing program. A position opened up at this organization that was social justice-related; I put my resume together, applied, interviewed, and was very lucky to be hired. I was a community health specialist, so my role was intervention and community outreach.

Because I was dedicated and very loyal to the work I was doing, I was promoted to coordinator of the program. This allowed me to work closely with the program manager and learn different things. I eventually became the program manager when that person moved on; I ended up working in that position for six years.

In 2002, my life then changed with the murder of Gwen Araujo, a transgender woman. It wasn't only that she was murdered, but the *way* she was murdered, that shook me. It really impacted me as a Latina. From then on, I decided that I needed to do whatever I could to organize and advocate for the issues affecting our community.

An opportunity came up for me to work at Children's Hospital in Los Angeles, as a coordinator for its transgender program. The hospital was very conservative with what they were doing, but I started being more vocal. I created a program called Angels of Change because there was a seventeen-year-old trans Latina woman who needed medical services but, because she was undocumented, was denied access. The program raised funds for trans people who didn't have a way to get services they needed.

Angels of Change began creating calendars with transgender youth models—which were shipped around the world to many different countries— and organizing runway shows. Doing this was how we raised money. I did this and other projects for eight years.

**That's wonderful! What ultimately led to the founding of TransLatin@ Coalition?**

In 2009, while I was working at Children's Hospital, there were a couple of national trans organizations advocating for the needs of trans people in general; but they weren't necessarily addressing the needs of trans *Latina immigrant* individuals at that time. I decided to organize a group of people to find out what we could do. We started with this idea of changing the structure, so we worked on policies to advocate for specific needs and issues, including housing and homelessness. We also worked on a study to identify issues faced by the community.

**Can you tell me about some of the programs the coalition runs, including the Center for Violence Prevention and Transgender Wellness?**

We started those programs after building our foundation in 2009. We were seeing that people who were trying to organize were still having trouble accessing basic services. In 2015, our national group got together to determine how we could address some of these issues. After receiving our first grant in 2016, we established the Center for Violence Prevention and Transgender Wellness: a place to help trans and gender-nonconforming people who are or have been victims of any type of violence, including sexual assault, domestic violence, harassment, hate crimes, etc. It is important for people to understand the violence that trans and gender-nonconforming people experience from our society, including structural and institutional violence, harms our ability to heal and be healthy individuals in mind, body, and spirit.

We also have a reentry program to help trans individuals who have been released from jail, immigration detention, or prison. We have a workforce program that helps connect people to jobs in their industry. We also have a drop-in center where people can just come and be, if that's what they want to do. They can watch television, read a book, watch a movie, or do whatever they like. We also have computers for their use. In addition, we provide clothes for people as part of our daily distribution program.

Currently, we are in the process of building our meal services. We also plan to have mental health services. We are the first trans-related organization in Los Angeles to provide these services to the community; we provide a space where people can come and be safe.

*That's truly amazing. Thank you so much for getting those programs off the ground. You know, I saw a video interview where you talk about cutting off your hair after letting it grow very long. This seemed like an important personal action for you.*

It was a political statement. I shaved my head on stage this past June, for Trans Pride. The message was that we can do whatever we want with our bodies without society dictating what we can and cannot do. I offered my hair as a symbol. Obviously, my hair was part of my identity, and it is still part of my identity; but I wanted to offer that as a political statement. It was very impactful. Many people were crying. As I was having somebody shave my head, I also read a poem I wrote about how society treats us and how I'm able to navigate society with my allies.

*I can understand the power of that act. I wanted to also ask you in general about how you have so much joy in your activism. How are you able to stay positive in the midst of the constant struggles?*

The joy I have is within me. It comes from my spirituality. There are different things I do every day to remain humble, because I believe that being humble is one of the things that should be rooted in the work that I do. The work keeps me grounded; at the same time, it gives me the joy I need to continue. Doing this work can be very taxing on my life, my mind, and my body.

I have seen many activists and organizations come and go over the twenty years that I've been doing this kind of work. What supports me and helps me to continue to move forward is the fact that I believe in a higher power. I believe I am here for a purpose. Even though at times I may not know or understand my purpose, I know that whatever I'm doing is because of my purpose. My spirituality is what makes me happy.

If I could send a message to everyone, I would want to tell them that hope is one of the things that keeps us afloat. Hope is what we are able to see in the darkest moments, and it is hope that helps us eliminate the road of struggle, the road of unfairness, and the road of injustice. If we carry hope with us in our hearts and in our minds and through our actions, we will be able to change the landscape of our community and our society.

There is also a resilience we have as both individuals and as a community that will help us walk together to the other side and cross the bridge victoriously. As long as we don't lose hope and as long as we acknowledge our resilience and our strength individually and collectively, we can walk together to the end goal, which is the dream of our people. Liberation will not be possible if we do not liberate ourselves from the pain in our hearts, from the drama, and from the injustices that we continue to experience.

STACY RUSSO

# Sarah Rafael García

Barrio Writers / LibroMobile

www.BarrioWriters.org / www.LibroMobile.com

—

"When we read, we read as a community."

*Sarah Rafael García is the author of numerous articles, essays, and the books Las Niñas: A Collection of Childhood Memories (Floricanto Press) and SanTana's Fairy Tales (Raspa Magazine). She uses her writing and love of literature to promote social justice in her community-engaged activism and youth programs. Sarah's work is focused on eradicating racism and other forms of oppression by uplifting young people in her community and beyond. In 2009, she founded Barrio Writers: a program that provides college-level creative writing workshops for youth, resulting in the publication of an annual volume. Sarah also brings the powerful tools of books and information to her community through her bookstore, LibroMobile. Herein, she discusses her projects and how her early life has inspired her activism and writing.*

—

I tell people I'm from two valleys– the Rio Grande valley and the Orange County valley. I'm the first person in my family born in the United States. I was born in Brownsville, Texas, which is at the southernmost tip of Texas and meets the Mexican border. Across from Brownsville is Matamoros, Tamaulipas, Mexico, and that's where my parents were born. Initially, I grew up with both sets of grandparents being close by. Naturally,

Spanish became my first language. A lot of my early life contributed to what I ended up doing later. You have a lot of first-generation familial and cultural expectations revolving around the theme of the American dream. That's how my life started.

When I was about four years old, my parents decided to leave Brownsville. We moved to Santa Ana, California, in the late 1970s. Technically, I grew up in Santa Ana. My whole family is in Texas even now, but we claim Southern California as home because that's all we knew for many years.

We come from long lines of laborers. My grandfather was a Bracero worker. Many of my aunts and uncles picked throughout their childhood. I have an uncle who lives on the land on which he used to pick. I think my father's intention was to leave that environment to give us a "better life," in the sense of something *outside* of labor. He did so, wonderfully! He came to California and never told us he was a laborer. He dressed in his Sunday best to go to work. He came back smelling good and clean after work. It wasn't until he passed away in 1988 that we realized he was a laborer.

My dad worked at the *Orange County Register* newspaper for ten years. When my first book came out and people found out that my dad worked there, they would say, "Oh, that's why you became a writer." I would say, "No," but now, when I think back, I say, "Actually, yes, that *is* why I became a writer." My dad worked in a labor room at the paper. He started as a janitor and ended up pushing paper through the machines. When he passed away, he was a foreman. He was taking classes at Santa Ana College, the community college, to improve his English and get some classes under his belt so that he could be considered for a higher position. So, yes— I'm a writer because somebody else did the labor work before me.

**You mentioned Spanish being your first language. Can you tell me about your experience in schools in the U.S.?**

I didn't learn English until I started elementary school. Going through the American school system was very challenging for myself and my family because no one had really experienced it. During the few years my parents and other family members were exposed to it, it wasn't positive. Several of them dropped out and got their GEDs instead. When my parents arrived in the U.S., they were teenagers. They dropped out of school within their first year because of the ridicule and oppression they faced: not just from Caucasian residents, but also from other Mexicans— who knew English.

These experiences caused my family to have a whole other level of expectation for me. They assumed that because I was born in the United States, I wouldn't experience or be exposed to any of those issues. They didn't stop to think about the fact that Spanish was the only language I knew. My first four years in elementary school were really hard, between my parents learning English and trying to preserve our knowledge of the Spanish language. It became a constant conflict at home and at school.

In the late 70s and early 80s, there weren't many language-emergent programs. I was rerouted through the

English as a Second Language (ESL) system. The ESL program took place literally whenever the ESL teacher got there. They would take the ESL kids out of class—which could be in the middle of math, history, or a quiz. This was a form of segregation, because everybody knew you needed a "special" class. My parents would fight against it every year, starting in kindergarten. I think it's because they went through that that, in fourth grade, my parents coached me to lie to my teachers. They said, "When they ask you what your first language is, say English."

That was probably the first time in my life in which I realized I had to lie or pass to be successful in the United States. I had to deny my culture and deny where my parents were born. That became something I thought was normal— to assimilate.

My dad was attempting to do the same. We would see him practice his English every time he was up for a promotion. The whole point was to find a way to have no accent. We thought it was normal to not be proud of who you are, but to try to blend in and not cause any problems. I mastered it. I now have an accent when I speak Spanish versus when I speak English. Few people can recognize that Spanish is my first language.

**How did you become a writer, and how did this lead to your different projects and activism?**

My parents were always huge supporters of books. The library was not only a place for us to check out books, but it was also our babysitter when my mom had to go grocery shopping. It was the only way for us to afford books. Through this, we were quickly exposed to summer reading programs. I grew up reading Judy Blume and *Little Women*. I couldn't tell you why I read those books back then. I can tell you now: it's because the characters were all women. I didn't read my first Mexican-American author until my senior year of high school. It was Richard Rodriguez's *Hunger of Memory*, which reflected what my dad went through.

I have a collection of books that my dad signed for me. Growing up, that's what saved me. That's what got me through his early death. Luckily, at the time, I had a bereavement social worker who knew I always had a big chip on my shoulder as a teenager. The counselor said, "You're never going to talk to me. Here's a journal. Write all of your feelings out, and maybe one day you'll talk to someone." She changed my life. Without that experience, I would have never become a writer.

After high school, at Irvine Valley College, a community college, I had my first Mexican-American teacher, Lisa Alvarez. Through her, I was exposed to Writers of Color. One day, she approached me after I had written a couple of essays for her class. She said, "You should consider becoming a writer." I just thought, "No, I have to go get a job. I have to make money. I have to help my family. I don't have time to be a writer." I just let it go.

Out of college, I became a social worker. I discovered all of the bureaucracy behind it. Then I went into marketing. For about eight years, I worked in national marketing for the American Heart Association, for construction companies, and education companies. I got fed up. I was exhausted of all of the expectations of the

American dream. I went to teach English in Beijing, China, for a year and a half— from 2004 to 2006. I did this so that I could write. I didn't know what I was going to write. I had no idea. I didn't even know if I was a good writer. I wrote journal entries about my first twenty memories of growing up with my father, because I wanted to capture what we had. I wrote the whole book in China, and I came back to the U.S. in 2006. My goal was to get published. I gave myself two years. I ended up getting published after *exactly* two years. When my first book came out, it was really empowering!

I relocated back to Santa Ana to show my community who they made and where I came from; if this girl beat all of the odds and was able to get published, anybody can do it! I came back with that idea. I started presenting on school campuses. I realized the words that I heard growing up are still the phrases that teachers are using on campus like, "Don't speak in Spanish. Sit down. Be still. Stop talking." I walked out of one presentation thinking, "Oh my God, my little book isn't going to do anything. These youth need an outlet. They need a different way to approach things and see things." That's how Barrio Writers came to be.

**Tell me more about Barrio Writers.**

My first book was released in 2008, and by June 2009, we started Barrio Writers. I didn't want to be another adult telling young people what they have heard their whole lives. Everybody is telling them what to do, but no one is giving them the resources or the tools to do it. I wanted to give them the tools.

Barrio Writers is for ages thirteen through twenty-one. We offer free college-level creative writing workshops to youth. Originally, it was a ten-week program; now, we have condensed it into a one-week program. They produce more writing in one week than in ten! The workshops are held in the summer. Once the youth participate in the five-day workshop series, they get to submit their work for publication, and then they present their work at a live reading.

Barrio Writers is completely grassroots. It exists through community collaboration. We solely discuss Writers of Color and LGBTQIA+ writers. We also mentor youth to become workshop facilitators themselves. When we read, we read as a community. There is no hierarchy in the workshop. Everyone is on a first-name basis. We're not there to tell them where to sit or to be quiet. We spend the first half of the workshop reading, deconstructing, and critically examining. During the second half, we learn style, and they create their own work. The youth also get to share their work. They gain empowerment through positive and constructive criticism. We always end the day by telling them something they do well and one way in which they can improve.

We started out as one chapter in Santa Ana. We now have ten chapters. We have three in California and seven in Texas. Each chapter is run by volunteers. By this point, there have been hundreds, if not thousands, of youth involved.

Each year, we publish a volume with writings from the workshop. Everyone who participates is included, unless they do not want to be. They also create a bio that is published. I always tell folks, "Your job is to write. My job is to publish." They all receive a copy, and we sell copies to help fund the program. The first five editions were self-published. When we started a chapter at Stephen F. Austin State University in Nacogdoches, Texas, their press expressed interest. Since the sixth edition, they've been publishing Barrio Writers— which is great, because we no longer have to raise the funds to publish the book!

**That sounds so empowering. How did your work as an activist also lead to the creation of LibroMobile?**

LibroMobile came as a response to the last bookstore closing in Santa Ana. The mission is to bring literature that is relevant to the community. The focus is on Writers of Color, LGBTQIA+ writers, marginalized voices, women's voices, mental health, and local writers and artists. At first, I decided to set up a mobile bookstore because of the problem bookstores face with rent and space. I wondered, "How can I counter the idea of needing to have funds upfront to pay for space and still offer books in our community?" Delilah Snell, from a business called Alta Baja Market, had this planter on wheels for which she had no use. I looked at the planter, and I said, "That's a bookmobile." I thought I could put books on this mobile thing and take it out to the community. I would have books for sale on a sliding scale and have a little free library for people who can't afford books.

In the process of doing all of this, I discovered that there's a law in Santa Ana forbidding the sale of any products on the street. You can get a license to sell food and drinks, but I could not get a business license to pop up on a corner and sell books. I started looking for ways to do it. I partnered with an art organization during the city's monthly Art Walk, and I set up for special events. Then I applied for a city grant and got it. I was able to hire a local female welder named Diana Markessinis to retrofit the planter into a bookmobile.

The bookstore has evolved over time. What started out as a bookmobile for 100-200 books transformed into a stairway that held about 300 books. From the stairway, it has turned into a 300-square-foot warehouse with over 1,000 books, along with the bookmobile that still goes out to events. We have books on a sliding scale, as well as free books and $1, $3, and $5 sections. We also have a little free library that's on its own wheels. Our bookshelves have books that cost under $20. Although we do have new books and those are sold at full price, we try to only keep books that are $20 and under.

LibroMobile initially started with support from Red Salmon Arts, which is connected to a bookstore in Austin, Texas, called Resistencia Bookstore. It was originally started by Raul R. Salinas and is now maintained by two Queer Women of Color, Lilia Rosas and Tañia Rivera. Raul is an Indigenous Chicano ex-con who started a safe space for folks who were being immersed back into the community from the prison complex. He extended the space to youth and, eventually, to everyone else in that community. He was an inspiration behind LibroMobile, so we call him the Padrino of LibroMobile. He's our godfather.

Now that we have the space, we are open most afternoons. I have volunteers and part-time workers. In addition to books, we sell art by local artists. They keep 100% of their proceeds. Artists from surrounding areas, like Los Angeles, receive a 70/30 split in order to create equity for local artists. We continue to provide a space for Artists of Color to gain exposure.

The main audience I'm reaching on a daily basis at the bookstore are Spanish language readers. We have not had one single day on which someone doesn't come by and ask for a book in Spanish. We can't keep the Spanish books on our shelves! They are looking for books they can take home and call their own. It's not the hipsters and the affluent people coming into the bookstore on a daily basis. It's people in my community who are looking for books that are relevant to their daily lives. My focus is on them. That is the heart of my activism.

### How do you stay positive with your activism?

Honestly, I love giving away books to Spanish-speaking children and teens. It reminds me of my own childhood, and the gift my parents provided each time they encouraged us to read. I believe we are raising adults rather than children. We need to treat them like the adults we want them to be. We should give them the opportunity to see themselves on a book page and as role models for others. We should give them a space to be critical yet also one to make them feel empowered to take action and create change—books offer just that. They allow readers to gain new perspectives. Books challenge stereotypes and inspire dreams of a better world. I can't pretend I don't have days that I feel muted and defeated.

On those days, writing keeps me positive. I too need to purge my thoughts and create a better world through characters that embody my culture and gender and that one day will be read by people who need to see themselves in the pages of a book, too.

STACY RUSSO

# Michelle Habell-Pallán

Women Who Rock

Content.Lib.Washington.edu/WWRWEB

—

"Our activism is centered on stories based on building
community around culture and joy."

*Michelle Habell-Pallán is a professor of Chicana/Latina Studies
in the Department of Gender, Women & Sexuality Studies at the
University of Washington. She is the first Chicana to receive the
rank of full professor at the university. Michelle's books include
Loca Motion: The Travels of Chicana/Latina Popular Culture and the coedited Latino/a Popular Culture, both published by
NYU. She also co-authored American Sabor: Latinos and Lati-
nas in US Popular Music | | Latinos y Latinas en La Música
Popular Estadounidense, published by University of Washington
Press. With her colleague at the University of Washington, Michelle
founded the Women Who Rock: Making Scenes, Building Communities oral history archive. The archive was created to "bring together scholars, musicians, media-makers, performers, artists, and
activists to explore the role of women and popular music in the creation of cultural scenes and social justice movements in the Americas
and beyond." In this interview, Michelle discusses her early life in
Los Angeles; her educational journey, which included studying with
Angela Davis; the creation of Women Who Rock; and the importance of joy and relationships for an activist life.*

—

I grew up in a big Mexican-American family. I was born

at a new Kaiser hospital in the city of Bellflower in Southern California. My dad was working as a paramedic, so I believe he didn't have to pay for me to be born there. We actually lived in Southeast Los Angeles County in Huntington Park. My grandmother had a tortilleria on Florence Avenue, deep in the heart of Southeast L.A. The tortilleria was called San Antonio, after her patron saint.

My grandmother had learned the business from her big sister, who opened one of the first tortillerias in East L.A. They crossed the border at Texas with my great-grandmother and their other siblings around 1919 or 1920. They came to the U.S. from Aguascalientes in central Mexico due to the Mexican Revolution of 1910. It was something like a penny to cross over, back then. There was really no border, so you could go back and forth. When they first came over, they picked cotton; but my grandma was only five years old, so it really hurt her fingers. It was a difficult time. My grandmother started going to elementary school in Texas, and they would hit the kids if they spoke Spanish. My great-grandmother somehow got the idea to go to Los Angeles because there was work there. She was a widow, and I think she had five or six kids. I don't know how these ladies did it! My great-grandmother had a little food cart at the time and would attract customers with the smell of the food cooking.

When they arrived in California, they met an African-American family that had a boarding house in the Los Angeles area. They hired my great-grandmother to be a sous chef. Obviously, this was in the days of segregation, so this was a boarding home and a restaurant for Black folks. During her time there, she learned to make Waldorf salad and all kinds of U.S. food. Later on, my uncle also had a bakery on Rosecrans, in the Compton area. My family has always been connected to the Southeast L.A. County area.

My dad, interestingly enough, is a white Catholic man from Indiana. He became part of the family, but we didn't really see much of his family, since they were so far away. Both families were against my parents' marriage at the time because it was seen as a "mixed" marriage. The only reason the wedding was allowed to happen was because they were both Catholic. I ended up growing up in Downey, which was a completely different world and very white. However, we would go back and forth all of the time to Southeast L.A. to see my grandma.

### What was it like growing up in Downey?

The musical group The Carpenters were from Downey, and they really represent what Downey aspired to be, which was to maintain its whiteness even though it was surrounded by Communities of Color. With my name being Michelle Habell, I looked white on paper; but, when the teachers saw me, that was a whole different thing, since I could never pass as white. I look very Mexican. I look like my mom. Even as a little kid, I had the sense that my last name gave me some kind of advantage; but that didn't stop the teachers from treating me differently, as one of the Brown kids. Kellyanne Conway is kind of an archetype of some of the girls with whom I went to high school.

To get through high school and all of those teachers, I would listen to the radio. Music saved me. I listened to a radio program called the Dr. Demento Show. My radio was a salvation in the life that I had at that time. My mom's side of the family was the good, fun part, while the bad was growing up in Downey. Punk rock and ska were my salvation, and how I survived high school. I realized I was never going to fit in, so I just went all out the other way!

### What did you do after high school?

I first went to Long Beach State University and then transferred to San Diego State University. I majored in English. I ended up volunteering for the college radio station, so music was always there with me. I also had my own show. Once I graduated, I decided I would apply for graduate school in literature at UC San Diego; but, if I didn't get in, I would just go back to L.A. and start a band. I ended up getting into grad school, though.

This was around the time when cultural studies were starting in the U.S. The literature department at UC San Diego was really progressive and had been shaped by Marxist literary scholars. Angela Davis was connected to the department, and she had completed her PhD there. So, I found myself within a radical intellectual tradition with activist scholars, and it just blew my mind! I started to read scholars who were coming out with books about politics and music and activism. I also discovered third world feminism and Women of Color feminism. I read Audre Lorde and Toni Morrison. Everything I was learning opened up a whole new world for me.

At this time, there was also a convergence happening. Queer Chicano performance art was exploding in L.A.

My advisors let me write about that and the artistic Chicano activism that was happening around L.A. My writing was coming from a Queer and feminist perspective. Somehow, everything came together for me there. I believe I was in the right place at the right time. It felt powerful, and I thought, "This is a whole other world, and I want to be part of this world. I'm going to make it my goal to be part of this." That's how I came to understand there was such a thing as a scholar activist. Still, I didn't really know what I was going to do with my life. I thought about how Angela Davis was at UC Santa Cruz, so I applied there for my Ph.D.

### What was it like when you were at UC Santa Cruz?

What was great with a scholar like Angela Davis is that she really encouraged us to work in collectives. We had a collective called Women of Color in Conflicting Collaboration. Some of us had come to graduate school from organizing. My dear friend Keta Miranda was older than we were at the time. We were in our twenties; she was in her forties. She had been a long-time, hardcore community organizer who decided to go to graduate school. bell hooks had been a part of the program also, but she had already completed her Ph.D. when I arrived. Still, her legacy was there. Gloria Anzaldúa was still connected to the Literature Program, and I got to meet her a few times.

We were a mix of young people and more experienced people in the collective. We were learning from each other about organizing. We had an interesting mix of hardcore activists from the day and those of us who were still trying to figure things out. I was lucky to be in this mix of incredible women and feminist, activist scholars. I was always interested in culture, so my activism was rooted there. At this time, there was also a new movement in literary scholarship that looked at providing a voice to cultures, communities, and people living on the southwest border of Mexico and the United States.

When I finished my dissertation, I was hired at Arizona State University right off the bat to teach Chicana feminist studies, which was a powerful department on the campus. This was in 1996. There was a little boom in the economy, and universities were hiring; but then, everything went flat.

**How did you become a professor at the University of Washington?**

I loved the students in Arizona, but I couldn't deal with the weather, so in 1998, I applied for a Chicano studies position at the University of Washington. I'm now a full professor there. Proudly, but also sadly, I'm the first Chicana, Mexican-American to be promoted to full professor at the university.

**Wow. That sure says a lot about the academic world.**

**How did the creation of the Women Who Rock archive come about?**

My colleague from the University of Washington, Sonnet Retman, and I had wanted to organize a conference around women and music at the university for years. We couldn't get funding, so we were a little bitter about it. However, later on, we were able to recruit a graduate student named Martha Gonzalez, along with her husband,

Quetzal, and their son. Martha was recruited into the feminist studies PhD program to write about the son jarocho fandango music tradition from Veracruz, Mexico. Martha was the singer of the beloved Los Angeles-based Chicano band *Quetzal* that shared the same name as her husband. The grant funding that we received at that time allowed us to work on creative projects between the Experience Music Project Museum in Seattle and the university.

Martha's husband, Quetzal, was hired to help promote programming between the university and the museum. He knew all about the incredible art scene I had written about in the 90s, since he had been part of it. He was the son of organizers and had been organizing with the Zapatistas, a community in Chiapas, Mexico that has been struggling for self-determination since an uprising in 1994. He was just an incredible person. One day, I complained to him about the conference and our proposals always getting rejected. His response was, "Just plan to do it anyway. People who get it will show up." I wasn't sure about what he said but eventually, it worked out.

After submitting a new proposal that was successful, Sonnet and I, along with graduate students, were able to establish the archive Women Who Rock. Initially, the project began as a class centered around the idea of women in music and politics, for undergraduate and graduate students. The projects focused on recording the oral histories of local women in music who had never really been interviewed. Oral history is a method of gathering and preserving the history and stories of individuals and communities through interviews. It just so happened that the University of Washington Libraries had a digital initiative at that time. Somehow, Quetzal put us in touch with Ann Lally, the librarian in charge of digital collections. We proposed that the library take the oral histories that the students were recording and preserve them. She responded with, "Great. No problem." We couldn't believe it. That is where the archive of the recorded histories continues to be maintained.

The students did their interviews and. eventually, they also made documentaries, including one about Home Alive called *Rock, Rage, & Self-Defense*. Home Alive was one of the first feminist self-defense organizations organized by women musicians after the murder of the Seattle musician Mia Zapata, the singer of the punk band The Gits. She was raped and murdered while going home from a show. After it happened, Mia's community in Seattle came together and created Home Alive. It was an incredible organization that lasted about ten years. Our students interviewed women who were part of that, and then they created a whole mini-documentary that screened at different festivals in Europe and in the U.S. That was exactly the kind of activism we envisioned and hoped for by creating the class.

### How would you describe this type of activism?

It is an activism that involves people from marginalized communities in all aspects: as organizers, oral historians, students, and individuals whose stories are recorded and archived. We work to break down hierarchies between the university and people who may not have access to the university. We believe we all have the power to teach.

Our activism is centered on stories based on building

community around culture and joy. It is activism for everyday people, especially those who are burnt out. I believe the new way to live activism is to make it about joy, getting together, taking care of each other, and sharing our stories. What we need is a healing and regenerative activism that says, "Let's just get together." We need to share stories and hang out together to build social movements. That is what the Women Who Rock archive has become since the very first class.

The archive is not just about musicians anymore. Musicians are one part of a scene, but scenes have their own ecologies. The specific scenes we are interested in are ones with artists and musicians who use music as a means of social justice. We archive the stories of musicians, advocates, and activists, as well as the stories of people who are behind the scenes. To be an activist does not mean you have to be out in front. We want to make sure that we recognize the people that support those at the front because sometimes they get overlooked. In addition, we also collect the stories of scholars, journalists, zine creators, and other media makers who are helping to make sure the history of marginalized communities within music scenes is recorded. We capture the making of scenes and the building of communities.

It is a transformative lens when you begin to look at what makes up a scene versus who is at the front of a scene. It takes a whole bunch of different, interrelated actions, and practices to make the scene happen. Every action or practice is as valid as the next, though some might be more visible than others.

*The original project has now become much more*

*than an archive at the university library. What are other activities that have evolved from this project?*

Women Who Rock has also expanded beyond the local area where we initially began. We had a graduate student, Kim Carter Munoz, who was collecting oral histories in Mexico by interviewing Indigenous musicians. When I saw her collection, I was very inspired. Her work made Sonnet and I realize that we had to do this work in Seattle and beyond.

We also came to understand that an oral history archive is only useful if it is building community. This means people having face-to-face interactions around it or using it in some way. Every year, we have the (Un)Conference that teaches an aspect of the archive or collects material for the archive or shares the archive. That's how we keep it alive and also build community. The full title of our project is Women Who Rock: Making Scenes, Building Communities. The vision has been influenced by the Zapatista movement in how we use music as a way of forming links and connections.

An important and powerful part of movements for emancipation and social justice is how you can come together by using the resources that you have. We understand this as *convivencia*. You can build a project around the vision of the people who are in it and the skills they have, rather than imagining a project that needs particular skills. Therefore, we use the skills we have to shape our projects. This is a form of activism that gives people hope. For example, maybe you like to cook and want to build community and activism around cooking or food justice, so maybe all your activism revolves around hosting a weekly potluck for your community. It is important to form community in a world that constantly wants us to be separate from each other.

*What you have created through Women Who Rock is very beautiful and inspiring. I can hear the joy in your voice, yet earlier you mentioned the racism you experienced and then the difficulty you encountered in the academic world to secure funding for your project. How do you stay positive in your activism?*

We will not be able to survive the reality of what is happening in the world if we feel guilty about sharing, having fun, and being joyful because that is what it means to live. That is how I stay positive. I'm not saying that we ignore reality, but we must continue to participate in the world we want and do things that make us happy as a means to survive. For those of us who have more privilege than others, we need to use our privilege and learn from others who are not as privileged to build together to make a more just world.

We cannot feel guilty about experiencing joy when the world is on fire. If we give up our joy, they've completely won. I am not talking about a joy related to money or things we own. It's about finding joy in being together. It's about our relationships with each other and Mother Earth. If we don't understand that our relationships bring us joy and sustain us, we will not be able to survive. I want to continue to live a life of joy.

For anybody who wants to be an activist now, I would tell them to look for the joy. Look for joy in what you do and share that feeling with other people. To share one's activism is a political act. It is an act that is going to help us build the world that we want.

**Hilary Kinavey**

Be Nourished

www.BeNourished.org

—

"If we keep centering the most marginalized people, we will all get free."

*Hilary Kinavey co-founded the Portland, Oregon-based Be Nourished with Dana Sturtevant. The manifesto for Be Nourished, a body-positive organization, provides several "We Believe" statements, including "We believe body liberation is a vital part of creating a fair, just, and equitable world" and "We believe people who are willing to view bodies through a compassionate and inclusive lens will change the world for everyone." In this interview, Hilary discusses how feminism has historically not addressed body-image issues well, but has instead continued to promote dieting, thinness, and restrictive ideas of beauty. She also talks about her work with Be Nourished, her desire to eliminate weight bias in the healthcare field, and the concept of "intuitive eating" as an approach to healing our relationship with food and liberating all of us from body oppression.*

—

I grew up in California, in a family that was quite liberal and progressive— especially in regard to issues around equity, racism, and inclusion. It was a regular part of my family's rhetoric to talk about these things. My parents prided themselves on being hippies. They were pro-demonstration and supported most of the stances I took.

Our shared identity around being liberal and progressive created a sense of belonging; but there was certainly still a lot of stress in my family, due to addiction and other things. Unfortunately, my dad's addiction was a big part of our family life that never really got addressed. Still, he was also someone who I could count on for support in my alternative opinions.

My dad was a beloved English teacher. A lot of what I grew up believing or thinking were things that he taught to his students and, probably, came from literature. My mom was a businessperson in San Francisco in the 1980s, when the AIDS epidemic was particularly strong. She was an advocate for many people there and had many gay friends and business partners. The experiences she had during that time tremendously impacted her– and us.

When I was nine years old, we moved to a more conservative suburb. In this new neighborhood, as someone who was activism-oriented, I felt less of a belonging. I remember being in my government classes and discovering that I was the only person against the death penalty. It was a confusing time for me; but, ultimately, the experience strengthened my identity and commitment to having a voice and speaking out when I felt something was harming people.

**How did you begin your journey towards becoming a therapist?**

I zeroed in on becoming a therapist when I was very young— in junior high, at least, if not younger. I wanted to go to college. I went as far north as I could, to the most liberal school I could find, which was Humboldt

State University. I lived there, in the Redwoods, for four years. I found myself leaning towards women's studies and sociology, so I studied these as a minor and received a bachelor's degree in psychology.

I remember having a strong feeling in high school that I wanted to be of service. When I got to college, I became active. There was a program there called the YES House. It allowed students to join and run social service programs. I became a director for a program that served teenage parents in the community, in which we paired college students with teenage parents for mentorship and support.

In addition, I coordinated the feminist Clothesline Project, which brings awareness to violence against women. I also got a job working at a crisis hotline for youth. I spent most of my time in college getting my degree and doing social service work. I went to graduate school at Portland State right after I finished my bachelor's degree. I earned a counseling degree by the time I was twenty-two or twenty-three. I was very driven, and suppose I still am!

*That is extraordinary to have your graduate degree at such a young age. How did you eventually get involved in the work that you do with Be Nourished, which is both unique and focused?*

I remember being a teenager and thinking about my future career. It was clear to me that I wanted to own a clinic in which women were safe to talk about their bodies. I don't know why. I just recall that being really important to me. My relationship with my own body was somewhat flawed. I was fortunate not to have developed an eating disorder, but I definitely struggled with what we call body image, and discomfort with not having a thin body. I have an average, small-fat body. I still had a lot of body privilege, but I didn't have all of the privilege that comes with being thin. I knew this to be true.

I wanted there to be different conversations about bodies. I was raised around a lot of feminism. All of the women in my family identify as feminists. Yet they all dieted, just like everyone else did. They weren't necessarily negative about my body, but there definitely was the sense that we could all improve and work on our bodies. Because I grew up cemented in feminism, I did not understand how the two went together. There was an inherent disconnect between dieting and feminism that was never spoken about; I believe the women in my family didn't have the language to discuss it, much like the culture doesn't. I was kind of alone in sitting with the discomfort around it.

In *Tiny Beautiful Things* by Cheryl Strayed, she writes, "This is feminism's one true failure, that we've gathered the agency and the accolades in so many areas, and yet we've never stopped caring about the size of our ass." We have been duped. Consider that one of the first beauty pageants started the year after women got the right to vote.

When I finished graduate school, I was so tired of my body hate and loathing. It felt incongruent with everything else I stood for, and yet I hadn't found fat acceptance. I hadn't found a narrative about inclusion of bodies, because we attach such a strong and false health rhetoric to it. I was very lucky to find a therapist who spoke the language of intuitive eating, which is an approach to healing one's relationship with food and one's body. I found a book by Caroline Knapp titled *Appetites*. In *Appetites*, she discusses the relationships between culture, women's bodies, and eating disorders. That book helped me build some bridges I had been trying to find for a long time. Once I understood, I couldn't go back. I was angry that this conversation hadn't shown up at all in graduate school. Learning about eating disorders was completely optional. It still is for a lot of people in counseling programs.

I was upset that the pathologizing of bodies still happened in counseling. It happened all over my field, just like it happens in the medical profession and other places. I became very passionate about changing that narrative, and I started a private practice. Around this time— possibly fifteen or seventeen years ago— people in Portland were just beginning to have weight-loss surgery more regularly. People were able to get insurance coverage for it. You could second-mortgage your home and just opt for it. I got calls from women who recently had the surgery. They may have lost 50 or 100 pounds, and they had similar questions, such as "Why do I still hate my body?" "Why don't I love myself now?" "Why am I so angry about how the world's responding to me?" "Why am I so obsessed with the Food Network Channel?" "What is going on here; why didn't this fix it?" Those questions have really been the foundation of my work, for the rest of my career.

**How did this lead to the foundation of Be Nourished?**

After being in private practice for several years, I was asked to join a health clinic because the clinic wanted to focus on disordered eating and related issues. I joined and met Dana Sturtevant, who is now my business partner. She's a dietician/nutritionist. She's also a motivational interviewing trainer. She and I were both coming into this conversation about hope at every size and body oppression around the same time. We started offering groups together at the clinic. We found that we were exploring some of the same questions and starting to speak the same language. It was a great relief, since I hadn't yet met many practitioners out there who were thinking that way.

That clinic imploded due to some management issues, so Dana and I had a quick decision to make. We decided to get a private practice space together. We came up with the tagline "Be Nourished," and that's where we started. Being in this business together has been very organic. We haven't necessarily followed any of the business planning and coaching rules until it became necessary recently. It has evolved in parallel with our own awareness, activism, and paths. Our work is centered around the incredibly wonderful community of clients who have come to us over the years.

Dana and I have sat with people together and individually for thousands and thousands of hours, having conversations about healing our relationship with food and body. We continue to have questions. How does this healing actually happen? What does it mean to heal in this culture that's filled with weight bias and in which there are all of these intersecting challenges to being able to claim your body for yourself?

The business has grown quite a bit in the twelve years we've shared it. In the last five years, it has evolved into training healthcare professionals on how to do the work of body trust, which is what we call the work that we do. We also do quite a bit of advocacy and activism, particularly within the eating disorder treatment community. We feel and notice that we have a pretty tremendous impact on people because the paradigm we're offering is fairly counter-cultural and counter to the ways people may have envisioned their healing. We help people take weight off the center focus and put a healing relationship with food front and center. The dieting culture has a significant impact on our ability to occupy our bodies.

We also don't believe that people have to pursue health to be deemed worthy or have belonging. We want people to be able to make or not make whatever choices they want about how to care for themselves, knowing that the emphasis that our culture and our healthcare field have had on lifestyle changes has really been an inappropriate focus. We know that the social aspects of health have a far bigger impact on wellbeing than this individual responsibility rhetoric. A focus on lifestyle changes or personal behaviors only impact about five to twenty-five percent of our overall health status. Social constructions of health and wellbeing impact us far more, including genetics, environment, toxins, oppression, stigma, and access.

### Do all genders come to Be Nourished?

Yes, historically we have primarily seen cis-gender women. We also see a lot of folks that are trans or gender queer, and we do have some cis men that come and see us, too. We know that trans folks are more at risk for eating disorders than even white women, so we are working really hard to make sure that our work stays as gender neutral and invitational as possible, because that population has virtually no services and research to support the process of their healing.

### Can you explain what it means to eat intuitively?

When we grow up in a dieting culture, we tend to source information about what to eat, how much to eat, and when to eat from outside of us. It's very heady. Most of us have lost connection with some inherent cues that come from our bodies, about what to eat, how to eat, when to stop, how much to eat, and all of those pieces. We're born intuitive eaters. We come into the world knowing when we're hungry, and when we're full; as we grow and have access to more food, we know what we like and what we don't like. There is a very intuitive process in our body. We can be trusted with food.

Then we start getting messages about food, including what is good food or bad food, what are the right times to eat, what's too much, or what's special food. All of these things start to shift our relationship with food, and it becomes more moralistic for a lot of us. Intuitive eating is a way of returning to our bodies' cues and signals as a way to inform us on our relationship with food. As we learn how to eat intuitively, we move toward reclaiming the relationship with food that we all once had.

It doesn't mean that we're all supposed to be one size, either. Intuitive eating is not a new diet. It's not about thinness. People may gain weight when they do intuitive eating, they may stay the same, or they may lose weight. That's not really the point. The point is about healing your relationship with food, honoring that bodies come in all shapes and sizes, and that we have far more body diversity than we recognize as normal and appropriate in our culture.

I am interested in the relationship between social justice and therapeutic approaches, and how those two can intersect more. I want to eliminate weight bias in healthcare altogether, but particularly, my focus right now is in the eating disorder field. I'm also interested in doing more activism in the field and using my voice to shift the way the field is conceptualizing peoples' bodies.

*How do you stay focused and rise out of any experiences you have from burnout in your work and activism?*

I think a lot about burnout. I experience more burnout when I'm not using my voice regularly. A few years ago, I had to minimize my private practice significantly and start using my voice because I was becoming very tired and disillusioned. I felt like I was becoming a vessel for collecting peoples' stories, and there were so many similarities between the stories that weren't being heard in the world. I needed to know that change was possible systemically and institutionally. I didn't want to be the only recipient of these stories. Being a part of change is what actually addresses burnout for me, more than what most people mean when they say "self-care."

So many people are coming into awakening because of the election of Trump and everything that has happened in the world in the last few years. I think this is a time that can be really ripe for a lot of change. It is hard to witness what is happening, but I'm also remaining hopeful that this means that we can create a world that is safer and just for more people.

Claiming our bodies is an act of resistance. Resistance does not always resolve oppression, but it does bring us closer to humanity and connection. As a white woman, it is most important that I help with access to resources and then get out of the way so that folks who have lived with marginalized identities can access healing on their own terms and in their own communities. If we keep centering the most marginalized people, we will all get free.

# Yago S. Cura

## Los Angeles Public Library / Hinchas de Poesía

www.HinchasDePoesia.com

—

**"We need to start publishing our own books and creating our own presses."**

*Yago S. Cura, a bilingual outreach librarian for the Los Angeles Public Library, is the co-editor of __Librarians with Spines__, a collection of radical essays related to social justice issues in libraries and the library profession. He also created the literary journal __Hinchas de Poesía__ to make the publishing of poetry more equitable and to eliminate the boundary between North America and Latin America through an understanding of one America. Yago has a bachelor's degree in English from Florida International University; a Master of Fine Arts in Creative Writing from the University of Massachusetts, Amherst; and a Master of Library and Information Science from Queens College. He discusses the impact of being a child of immigrants; a compassionate consciousness he received through his work as an educator in the jail system; and the inherent racism in the publishing industry against which he struggles.*

—

I'm very fortunate that my parents were immigrants to the United States. Without a doubt, this is one of the secrets to my success. My experience has also given me an understanding about immigration. In 1973, my parents came to the States from Argentina. My mother was very involved in several student movements that sprung up in Buenos Aires. Because of this, my parents feared being killed by the government in Argentina and wanted to go someplace where they could be safe. First, they lived in Stuttgart, Germany, for about a year; however, they were unable to get their visas. Owing to an aunt living in Brooklyn, they moved to New York.

My parents were avid readers, so I was raised in a house in which there were books all over the place. There was also no hierarchy for the books; for example, you could find books on Argentina's history on the same shelf as children's books. I really owe my love of books and reading to my parents.

I remember going to LaGuardia Community College with my mom when she was a student. I was just a kid, five or six, so this would have been around '79 or '80. I've since learned that my dad was able to earn a math scholarship to attend at a reduced rate, or on a tuition waiver; but he still couldn't attend, because of his need to work to provide for the family. My father is a jeweler and continues to work despite being beyond retirement age. People automatically think that being a jeweler equates to having lots of money, but it does not. My father has always been committed to making an honest living, but I certainly did not grow up with any kind of opulence. There was a lot of love, however. I always felt that my parents loved me.

Unfortunately, life's circumstances did not permit my mother to complete her education. Therefore, I became the first person in my family to graduate from college. I almost feel like I kind of went overboard. From '93 to

'97, I went to Florida International University, and I received a BA in English. From '99 to '02, I received a fellowship at the University of Massachusetts, Amherst, and in 2002, I received my MFA in Creative Writing, with a focus in poetry. I was really fortunate to study with Martín Espada and Tomaž Šalamun. However, there were several other famous poets who taught at that school to whom I don't care to give any advertising because they proved themselves to be very small-minded and very racist. There were three or four Writers of Color in a program of sixty-five writers. I learned from experiences there to be careful what you put out; be careful who you think is on your side; and be careful of how you play with people who are scared, actually petrified of what you may be able to teach them.

I also have an advanced certificate in secondary education from Lehman College. In 2007, I won a Spectrum Scholarship through the American Library Association that allowed me to complete my second master's degree in Library Science from Queens College in 2009.

I kind of had a mission to use education to hopefully get rid of future obstacles. Some friends would say I was one of those eternal students; however, I don't have an important last name or a trust fund. How could anyone slight someone for wanting to try to better their position in a country that is hyper-capitalistic and highly dependent on stratifications?

*What has your professional journey been like?*

After grad school in Amherst, Massachusetts, I moved back to New York. The only work I could find was adjunct teaching positions. I taught for about a year at Kingsborough Community College, but I learned quickly how pitiful of an existence that is.

Although I had my MFA, I didn't have a published book. No one tells you that people don't give a crap about your MFA unless you have a book. I decided I needed some kind of insurance if I didn't want a salary that was going to fluctuate wildly semester to semester. As a teacher, you are at the mercy of the English Department chair liking you, and whether they think how you teach is sound.

I ended up going into the New York City Teaching Fellows program in 2004. I taught high school for three years and then transitioned to completing my degree in Library Sciences. During my last year of teaching high school in New York, I met my wife. We were both teaching in the Bronx; unfortunately, the school I taught at was highly impacted by cocaine. Cocaine was sold in and around the school and in the neighborhood. Before this time, I didn't know the first thing about life in the inner city; this was a wake-up call for me, in terms of realizing some of the privileges I had as a child and teen.

In 2008, I got married, and my wife became pregnant a couple of months later— while we were living in a small, one-bedroom apartment in Harlem. Shortly thereafter, we decided to move to Los Angeles. My wife had grown up in South Central Los Angeles and had a lot of family in that area.

When we arrived in California, I tried to get full-time employment with the Los Angeles Public Library. It was difficult because there was a lack of funding at the time. They offered me a part-time job, but I turned it down. I would not have been able to make a living in Los Angeles on the salary I was offered working half-time. Instead, I accepted a job with John Muir Charter School, which offered an education program for incarcerated youth. I worked at the Men's Central Jail and Century Regional Detention Facility, as well as the large Twin Towers facility.

My students were eighteen- to twenty-four years old. The program's goal was to prepare them for the California High School Exit Exam. The majority of my students had a fourth-grade reading level when I started working with them, and, within just a few months, they were able to pass the exit exam! The sixty-five-percent passing rate was truly an achievement.

My experience in Los Angeles has been a blessing. It's taught me a lot about what it means to be a person who works for the community and what the limitations and pitfalls might be. You have to work within the confines of a particular organization and their values. During this time, I got to see a good portion of our county's fabled jail system and was privy to a lot of things that changed my mind about incarceration, education, rehabilitation, and what we mean when we think of "punishment."

### What about these things changed for you?

Before I began teaching in the jail system, I was a lot more pro-death penalty and quicker to pass judgment and believe incarcerated people put *themselves* in their situation. After a few years of teaching in the jail system, and after my experiences working in South Central and the Bronx, I've become more open to understanding that, yes, while people make decisions that are sometimes wrong, how are we, as a society, making sure that all people have access to better decisions? For example, if we want people to become active readers in places like the Bronx, how can we assume this will be possible if the only bookstore available to the area is a Christian one? If we want people in South Central to be digitally aware and use those types of resources, how can they be if there is limited or no WiFi available to use? Things that may be a given to us are still luxury items in these communities. These things are accessible if you have the money; if you do not, then, tough!

My perspectives really changed when I saw, with my own eyes, how segregation and redlining set some neighborhoods up to fail. It's a terrible thing to become aware of because the work to change it is daunting: How can these issues be fixed when everyone else is passing the buck and not taking responsibility to help when they can? This awakening has led me to ideas about how advocacy should be. For example, if there's something needed that is not accessible, and the county won't provide it, as an activist, you can reach out and collaborate with people to begin organizing and, ultimately, provide what is needed.

Let me give an example of how entrenched things are: The sheriffs charge the city $400 a day to transport *one* person to jail. If you do a simple extrapolation of that, then 100 people going to court on any given day is already $40,000. The County of L.A. runs nine facilities. Let's say 100 people at each of the nine facilities go into court on a given day—that is $360,000 per day! When I started to look at these numbers, I started to wonder how dedicated the city or the county could be to preventing people from going to jail. It's clear that this establishment is making so much money from the system even through small things, like the mark-ups of things sold to prisoners in the commissary. You can get three cups of ramen noodles for one dollar at a regular grocery store; each cup costs $1.18 at a commissary. *These small observations are really the tip of the iceberg.*

I've concluded that the county is not interested in stopping people from going to jail, and the county is also not interested in educating people that are in jail to make sure that they are not imprisoned again. It doesn't make sense for them to address these issues, because they *need* them to come back. It is really sad to think about.

***Thank you for sharing about your experiences and how these devastating realities changed your perspectives. Following this work, did you continue working towards your journey as a librarian in Los Angeles?***

I always entertained the idea of being a librarian— although the idea did not come to me as naturally as wanting to be a writer. Still, I was always researching different things and trying to figure out how they worked. However, I wasn't aware that I could pay rent or raise a family doing it, and, at first, I really had a shallow idea about what librarianship is. Like most people, I thought librarians read books all day. I also never saw a librarian who looked like me, so I think that also led me to believing I could not be a librarian. I remember when I told my students at the jail that I was going to be a librarian for the city. They responded with, "Mister, you're not a woman." There are so many stereotypes about librarians. Yesterday, someone came to the library, and he had to ask me twice whether I was a librarian because he didn't believe me. I want to tell people that a librarian can look like anyone and not just a white woman who's going to shush you. It could also be a Brown man telling you to keep it down.

When I worked in South Central, one of the things I loved was when the kids would come into the branch and see me at the reference desk, because I could speak to them in Spanish. I could talk to them in a language that they felt comfortable in and in which they wanted to speak. I would always recommend books that had characters that looked like them. This is really important for my son, also.

I used to be the Adult Services Librarian for the Vernon Branch Library. In 2017, however, I was promoted to the position of Bilingual Outreach Librarian. There are only six of us in the Los Angeles Public Library. I work as a liaison with organizations and anyone else who would like me to come down and speak about library services and materials. Today, for example, I'm going to the Culver City Menorah House to deliver books to some seniors; I'm also planning on a program for senior citizens later in the month with a social worker. As a librarian, I serve my community as a cultural worker.

*You are now also a published author. How did your book, Librarians with Spines, come to be?*

In 2014, one of my best friends from graduate school, James Foley, was killed in Syria while working as a journalist. Two years later, I got many of the writers who attended grad school with us together to work on a book based on a form of Arabic poetry (Ghazals) that we then published titled *Ghazals for Foley*.

This was the first time that I attempted to publish something. During the process, I taught myself about book publishing, including how to get a Library of Congress control number and an ISBN. I continued amassing knowledge on book publication from then.

My Facebook friend Max Macias, a librarian in Oregon, reached out to me one day about collaborating on a book. It was a completely organic and grassroots project that resulted in *Librarians with Spines*. The book includes radical essays written by exceptional librarians, many of whom are Librarians of Color. We set out to explore what contemporary librarians think about colonialism, feminism, multiculturalism, religion, race, intersectionality, and other social justice and equity issues. The topics covered also included cultural representation in children's book, whiteness in libraries and education, and classism in library science education and librarian culture.

From publishing this book, I uncovered that, in the publishing industry, many people talk the talk, but don't walk the walk. There are incessant and very real problems. For example, the difference between Penguin and I is definitely distribution and that they have a shit ton of capital. However, in reality, what makes a publisher is the ability to have an ISBN port and acquire a Library of Congress control number, which is a simple email request. Beyond that, it is basically about working with a designer that will lay everything in the book out for you, as well as being diligent in editing the content.

## Have you experienced specific negative things with the publishing world?

I recently got in a bit of trouble with *Library Journal*, which is a major periodical for reviews that is used by all types of libraries and librarians. I sent them a copy of *Librarians with Spines* a year ago and never received a response. We received no coverage. The reason is because the publishing industry claims that I'm a vanity press, but that is completely inaccurate. I'm not publishing myself; I'm publishing professionals working in the field who are writing about topics that most librarians either don't know about, don't know they can write about, or don't know it's safe to write about.

I also reached out to Small Press Distribution. However, because I publish books on social action, they completely ghosted me. For them to distribute you, I believe there is a $200 fee; even though I am willing to pay for the service and play the game to get our books distributed, they refuse to even answer my email!

The publishing industry in the United States can't have it both ways. It wants to get in on the slice of the pie and make money off of Writers of Color, but then work diligently to exclude people who may not have the capital or the connections to get a book properly distributed. U.S. publishers talk about diversity, but they don't actually work to fix it. A March 2016 article in *Publishers Weekly* provided information through responses to an October 2015 survey of the publishing industry that revealed 89% of the respondents self-identified as white. This same article commented on another publishing industry survey called the Diversity Baseline Survey, which was conducted by Lee and Low Publishers. This survey, which was released in January 2016, found the number in the publishing industry identifying as white to be closer to 79% and those specific to editorial departments in the industry being 82% white (Gross et al. 2016).

I firmly believe now that if Latinx and African-Americans really want to make a dent in this problem, we need to start publishing our own books and create our own presses. To combat the incessant racism and exclusion, we need to collaborate and create, because none of the mainstream publishers and distributors are doing anything to mitigate the problem.

*These ideas of creation and collaboration remind me of the work you did to create the literary journal* <u>*Hinchas de Poesía*</u>*. Can you tell me why you started the journal?*

There are many distinctions between North American and Latin American poetry, but the word "America" should be used to refer to both of the continents. I was inspired to embrace this point of view by Jose Marti's *Nuestra America* and his idea that North Americans and South/Central Americans are *all* Americans. Therefore, the original goal of *Hinchas de Poesía* was representation. I started the journal in the Fall of 2009. I wanted to make sure there is an equitable playing field, and I'm looking to extend the dialogue of what poetry is— and what it can be— in this country from a Latinx point of view. Whether it's a North American writer or a South American writer, to me, they're both American writers. Therefore, Latinx from North, Central, and South America are welcome to contribute to the journal if they are the Latinx diaspora or Latinx living in Latin American and Caribbean countries.

*Considering all of the issues you have commented on and the well-funded reality of these large machines, how do you continue to create and stay positive in your activism?*

For me, exercise is key. I try to play futbol every Sunday with the LA Futbolistas in Almansor Park.

*Cited Works*

Gross, A. Kirch, C., Patrick, D., and Rosen, J. (2016). Why Publishing is So White. *Publishers Weekly*: https://www.publishersweekly.com/pw/by-topic/industry-news/publisher-news/article/69653-why-publishing-is-so-white.html

**Beth Pickens**

Author / Arts Consultant

www.BethPickens.com

—

"I can do my part to build the world that I desire."

*Beth Pickens is the author of <u>Your Art Will Save Your Life</u> (Feminist Press), which can be described as a love letter of support, encouragement, and inspiration for artists. She is also the creator of the zine <u>Making Art During Fascism</u>. Beth's work as a consultant for artists and arts organizations stems from her lifelong understanding of the importance of art for her life, her community, and the world. She attended the University of Missouri at Columbia, earning a bachelor's degree in English and a master's degree in Counseling Psychology. Beth discusses her political awakening, the work she does for artists, and how she ultimately found her unique calling.*

—

I felt isolated and different as a teenager. In retrospect, a big part of that was because I was Queer, and there were no openly-gay or -lesbian people around me. This was before gay-straight alliances existed in schools. There was not a single openly-gay person in my world. I had these specific belief systems and political and cultural leanings, but I had no language to connect to and no one with whom to explore these ideas. There also no talk about feminism, which would soon become a really defining part of my life.

I grew up in Western Pennsylvania, right outside of Pittsburgh, in a small town. I was born in 1979, so my teen years were the last teen years before the Internet. I didn't have my first email address until I went to college. This was defining for me, because it was really hard to find culture and to connect with people. Even though I lived near a decent-sized city, I had limited access to it.

I also come from a family that had very little education. I was the first person in my family to graduate from college. My parents married very, very young and had children very, very young. I was a really curious young person, so I read a lot. I wanted to do things and be a part of things, but there was nothing around me.

*In your book, __Your Art Will Save Your Life__, you discuss the major impact art has had on your life. Considering the limited resources in your small town, when did you first experience art in this life-changing way?*

In 1994, I attended the opening of the Andy Warhol Museum. I was fifteen years old. This was a real turning point for me, because I saw a lineage of which I felt a part. At the time, my neighbor was an artist and art school teacher. She had this really interesting life! She was child-free, and taught art to junior high school students in public schools. She made a zine about cow paraphernalia called *The Moosletter*. As a teenager, in the early 90s, I was really into zines, because they provided a connection to the underground and counter-culture. I worked for her before I could legally work, and assisted with typing, collating, and mailing her zine. She had readers from all over the world, and she also had incredible taste in art.

That's how I learned about different artists and eras of art and culture. She told me that the Warhol Museum was opening up, and, before it even opened, I had a t-shirt for it. It was an early promotional t-shirt from 1993, and I still have it!

I gave an informational speech about the museum in either eighth or ninth grade, while anticipating the opening. It was a really big deal for me, because learning about Andy Warhol led me into all of these other things— such as the Velvet Underground, Nico, Valerie Solanas, as well as other types of art, music, and performance in New York. When I attended the museum opening, it was a pivotal moment. My mind cracked open with the realization that communities of people had been creatively doing things together for many, many years.

After that museum opening, I went back all of the time, and it led to learning about more art, music, and performance. I had this instinct that I needed to get out of town after high school, and I would be fine when I did. These experiences instilled in me the idea that there would be people whom I would relate to, somewhere. I figured there must be people of my age with whom I would have things in common. Even though my family was working class and not college educated, they suggested I should go to college; so, I did.

**What was your college experience like?**

I was in the top percent of my high school, so it made sense that I would go to college; but I was sort of on my own figuring out how. I didn't know anyone who had gone to college. This was like a whole new world for me.

I only knew about college culture from movies. I had this horrible high school boyfriend who told me about the University of Missouri in Columbia. He said everyone went there for journalism. At the time, I was considering becoming a journalist, after working on the school paper for a year.

Following his advice, I applied to the University of Missouri. I thought I would get in because of my good grades and SAT scores. I truly had no idea about what I was doing. I thought I wanted to be a writer. I didn't really know how a person makes a life.

The day before I started school, I met my soon-to-become best friend, who is still a very, very close friend in my life. She is now a professor of history at Georgetown. I discovered journalism was not for me in about one week, so I changed my major to English. Ultimately, those four years of college transformed me the way college transforms people. I was politically awakened. I learned about critical thinking, feminism, and gender studies. I found out I was queer. I studied abroad, living in China for six months to learn Mandarin. I started to think about the adult I would become, who I wanted to be, and how I would spend my life.

**When did your path change and lead you to counseling?**

I was planning to go into the Peace Corps after college, even though I felt I had no skills to offer whatsoever. Due to a health scare, I was rejected. I realized I needed a full-time job with health insurance, because I thought there was possibly something really wrong. As an undergrad, I worked at the university's women center, and that sort of helped spur on my feminist awakening. After graduation, it turned out they had a full-time job opening that I applied for and got.

This was a huge pivot. I ended up working there for the next six years. The women's center had a large number of counselors, so people around me were getting their graduate degrees in counseling psychology. The center also offered emergency counseling; before I considered getting my degree in counseling psychology, I did a ton of crisis intervention with students around sexual assault, eating disorders, conflict, money, depression, anxiety, and mental illness. I found I was very gifted at this type of work.

I really enjoyed the work I was doing. I also loved the women working at the center, who were studying to become therapists. I decided it could also be a career for me, so, while working there, I earned my master's degree in counseling psychology.

***What happened next, and how did you end up moving to California and working specifically with artists?***

Around 2004 or 2005, I started going to San Francisco every summer during Pride month, because I wanted to be around a huge queer art community. All of my favorite queer writers were living and working there. I would go to California and bring ideas back for programming at the university. I decided I needed to go live in San Francisco. I started applying for jobs out there when I was getting ready to graduate with my master's degree. I moved to San Francisco in July 2007.

Even though I was working in health and human services when I first got there, I immediately immersed myself in the queer art world. I asked this man who was a queer art fundraising guru to mentor me. He taught me how to do grant writing, and I started getting involved in a fundraising capacity for queer artists in my community. I asked the Queer Cultural Center if they would hire me, and they did. I became their managing director. I also became the managing director for a queer literary organization. I knew this was where I had to be. I needed to work for the arts. Everything else ultimately burns me out, but art never does.

In addition to grant writing for artists to raise funds in support of their work, I provide career consultation. I also work with individual artists and with arts organizations and provide them with strategic planning and fundraising.

***Can you tell me more about the idea of "compare and despair" in relation to artists, which you discussed in your book Your Art Will Save Your Life?***

Compare and despair is when we compare our lives to other people, which leads to unhappiness. When we do this, we are comparing our insides to another person's outsides. We don't really know what's going on in another person's life. We just project things onto them, but we do not know their interior life. Other people are also comparing their interior life to our exterior, and this comparing leads to despair. Social media facilitates compare and despair more than maybe any other thing in modern life. This is something that happens a lot in creative communities. It's inherent to being an artist, and it's something that has to be countered and unlearned.

**Tell me more about the critical self-talk and the interior voice you talk about with artists in your practice and in the book.**

One of the guiding principles of my practice with artists is that we have to deal with the interior and the exterior at the same time. It's important that we look at what's going on within us on the inside.

I like cognitive behavioral therapy techniques, which focus on examining thoughts that produce feelings and, ultimately, affect behavior. I enjoy helping others learn through different techniques about what their interior monologue is. What I mean by this is finding out what a person says to themselves all day; we're often really unconscious of the way we talk to ourselves and the interior tape that's playing all of the time. It is usually pretty toxic, which is highly typical for most humans. It can affect us negatively over time. We may be saying mean things for months at a time before we even become conscious of it. It's important that we use strategies to help us learn to observe our thoughts and how we talk to ourselves. This way, we can then interrupt those negative patterns and uncover more choices in how to heal ourselves.

**Before your book _Your Art Will Save Your Life_, you created the zine _Making Art During Fascism_. What was the inspiration behind this?**

The zine came from the immediate aftermath of the 2016 election and the ways in which my clients, as well as the artists and writers in my life, were flipping out; everyone I knew was flipping out, but artists and writers were flipping out in this very specific way. I kept hearing things over and over again that essentially boiled down to, "My art's not that important. I should stop doing it and do something else." I thought this was not true, for a lot of reasons.

I immediately started compiling a pamphlet of questions I was hearing from my clients and other people. I was creating a framework through which an artist could make decisions about how they want to proceed while maintaining their creative practice. I had something I put together within about ten days after the election. I started offering it for free. I also started a weekly gathering called Making Art During Fascism at a community art space in Los Angeles. This was a free drop-in social emergency response place for people who were overwhelmed after the election. It was intended for artists. A lot of non-artists also came to it, frequently. We used the zine as a way for people to make decisions about their particular position in life, including their social position, what they cared about, what resources they had available and didn't have available, and how they wanted to proceed.

I wanted to help people, especially artists, maintain their practices and see that their practices are valuable no matter what's happening. I wanted them to be able to make sustainable choices about their outward activism that would not lead to immediate burnout.

*This leads to something else in your work. You write about the importance of having a joyful life within the context of activism and even within the midst of awful things happening. How did you reach this belief concerning joy?*

An essential hobby in my life is reading about and thinking about death, which is a Buddhist practice. I find this a really helpful practice, because it keeps everything right-sized. It keeps things in perspective.

I use an app called WeCroak, which reminds you randomly, five times throughout the day, that you're going to die. When you get the reminder, you can click to read a quote about death. This reminds me each day that I am mortal, and I have this one life. What do I want it to be like? Who do I want to be? What do I want my life to be comprised of? What do I want my days to be filled with? How do I want to feel? Do I want it to get better?

Life is very short, and I have control over so little. However, I do have authority over how I spend my days, who I am, and what it feels like to be me. Taking responsibility for the things that I do have some power and influence over helps me let go of outcomes that are outside of me. I can do my part to build the world that I desire.

STACY RUSSO

## Lark Lo

### Blk Grrrl Book Fair / The Feminist Preschool / Black Kids in Outer Space

www.BlkGrrrl.com / BlackKidsInOuterSpace.com

—

### "I never really understood poverty and racism in Los Angeles until I got on a bus."

*Lark Lo's activism branches out into several areas that demonstrate a strong desire of eradicating injustice and oppression in different, yet interconnected, spaces. In 2014, she founded the Blk Grrrl Book Fair in Los Angeles. Now held in Brooklyn, the fair has a goal of documenting and empowering "the experiences of women and girls who are members of the African diaspora and living or have lived on the East Coast of the United States." This goal is met through writing workshops, readings, vegan community meals, and other activities. Lark has also been advocating for transportation justice for over a decade, which has included blogging and making videos regarding her experiences with bicycling and using public transportation. In another branch of her activism, as a special education teacher who became aware of the racist and sexist practices in early childhood education, she created a training program for school staff called The Feminist Preschool. The training focuses on issues of race, gender, and economic class, and helps educators to create supportive spaces that are free of oppression and open to possibilities for all children.*

—

When I was a child, I knew I wanted to have an exciting life. I liked TV, movies, entertainment, and reading. When the first Apple computers came out, my dad got me one with a printer. I started a little newspaper that was really a gossip rag. I think it was called the *Pink Lady's Gazette*.

My mom was a homemaker, and my dad worked as a photographer. It was a strange job. He is an artistic person, and his job was taking photographs for the post office's advertisements. This was probably one of the last available secure art jobs he could have gotten, since my dad was from the silent generation. He wasn't a baby boomer, so he managed to get the tail end of all of the good opportunities.

It's so strange to think back on my early life. I grew up in an all-Black neighborhood that was very stable. I had no idea it was unusual. I was born in the Koreatown area of Los Angeles and lived in the Ladera Heights neighborhood in Inglewood from a young age. The people who owned the liquor store, the butcher, the baker, my dentist, my doctor– they were all African-American. Most of the people were also Catholic and from Louisiana. I went to an all-Black Catholic school. At the time, I thought everyone who was Black was also Catholic!

When I was young, I imagined my life was boring; but now, I realize I was really lucky. I believe the racial issues in Los Angeles were a lot less pronounced then. When I went to college, all of a sudden, I became a Black person.

### *When you say you "became a Black person" when you went to college, what about that experience made you feel this way?*

When I was growing up, the Black community in Los Angeles was very strong. The Black middle class had an agency that I thought was everywhere. I have come to find out it is very rare. We had a bank, three newspapers, and three radio stations back then. Living in that environment, I had no idea that I was a "minority." I didn't know people had certain views. My parents sheltered me from racism. In some ways, this is positive, because I've always known how I'm supposed to be treated. There was never a period when I was treated badly or unfairly simply for being Black while I was growing up; because of this, I was very aware of the differences in how I was treated once I left my community and entered college.

I first went to college in UC Riverside. This ended up being a really unpleasant experience. It was the first time I was Black somewhere. I was in shock at the things that were being said to me. I thought, "What's happening here? Is this racism?" I remember being asked if I had a father. There was also an incident in which the school was going to auction off a student, for an event that was like auctions during slavery. I stopped that. I also led a protest to close down Greek Week because of Coors Beer being a sponsor, owing to the company's history of racism towards Mexican-Americans. The whole campus was shut down, and the president of the college had to come back from vacation. Coors sent a Black woman to talk to me, but I just walked out after telling them they didn't get it.

I decided to leave UC Riverside and relocated to Mount Saint Mary's, which is an amazing college. There was a variety of students from different ethnicities there, and we were all women. It was great. I studied philosophy there. Later, I went to Pacific Oaks in Pasadena and received my master's degree in human development.

**Following your activism work, I noted how vegan food is part of the Blk Grrrl Book Fair you founded. How did you become vegan?**

My family was always very healthful. My parents are vegetarian. My grandmother was one of the first people I ever knew who did yoga. Meat was not really a part of my life. I later became vegan when I was in college. Even though I call myself vegan, I like to say I'm a conscious eater. Being vegan is not just a diet, however; it's part of my life. Being vegan means that I'm trying to do the least amount of harm when I'm partaking in daily life. Veganism that is only about diet is not veganism, just like feminism that is not intersectional is crap because it fails to recognize interconnections.

I am also concerned about the payment and treatment of others. I ask myself, "Am I contributing to the exploitation of people?" I can't avoid everything, but I make choices to avoid causing harm to the best of my ability. My mom was always very political, including being inspired by Cesar Chavez and concerned about farmworkers. For years, we did not eat grapes.

**Tell me about the establishment of the Blk Grrrl Book Fair you started in 2014. What was the mission and inspiration behind it?**

I wanted to have something in South Central Los Angeles that was a big art event with dignity and agency. Events tend to be organized surrounding the perspectives of white men by default. I felt it would be great to have a gathering that was inclusive of everyone instead.

The idea for the Blk Grrrl Book Fair came from the Blk Grrrl Book Show I first created. During the show, I interviewed artists, writers, and a wide range of individuals who were involved with politics. I felt challenged about my Blackness continuously, so I used the show to talk about it and attempted to change people's perspective on what Black is. For example, there are really rich people and really poor people who are Black. There are Black people from the Caribbean, the continent of Africa, and many other locations. I wanted to expand the idea of what Blackness is in Los Angeles.

After the show, I thought of having a feminist book fair of which all women could be a part. If you identify as a woman, you would be welcome to attend. From its inception, the fair has been inclusive of everyone and open to nonbinary and trans women. The only people who asked if they could come, however, for some reason, were older white women. I don't know if that was because they felt weird about going or because they didn't want to go. Of course, it was open to them also.

Blk Grrrl has always been global, intersectional, and punk. I did not want the fair to be something where cis men picked which women were okay to participate. Instead, women chose who would be on the book fair panels, and, by doing this, it challenged how we label and do things. For example, at most events— even feminist events— I knew that people who picked the women for panels were men, and men would fund the events. My idea was to give women agency. Women organizing at the fair could put together a panel with whoever they would like, and I would provide them with the financial or technical support to be successful. We also see a lot of women on panels at events who do not have children. I believe the patriarchy likes women with no children, so they don't need to worry about childcare. I don't have children, and I don't believe having children makes you a woman. However, I definitely made sure that we had childcare. I think ours was one of the first events that had real, accessible, and plentiful childcare. It was not just lip service.

Different types of political groups take part in the fair, so there are tables with books that are feminist and race-conscious. The fair also hosts a film festival. The fair is about people creating things and putting their creations out there.

### How did your activism extend to include the foundation of the Feminist Preschool?

I started the Feminist Preschool in 2015 or 2016. During the day, I worked as a special education teacher for early childhood education. My class was made up of students who could get thrown out of school and preschool. My children were neurodivergent, neuroatypical, or on the spectrum of autism, so they acted in ways that some preschool teachers felt were not appropriate for an educational setting. I thought my students were fine! Some people don't know how to educate children with superpowers. No student was ever sent away from my class, of which I am very proud. As their teacher, I was able to get my students to figure out how to function in society. I would not focus on telling them they were doing things wrong. Instead, I would explain what they needed to know in a way that they understood.

While working in the educational system, I realized that a lot of the teachers were very sexist and racist in their practice. Because of this, I decided to develop a training program to teach educators how to ensure that their classrooms are free from sexism and racism. The training I provide is specifically for early child education centers, but I also hold trainings for churches and parents.

There were already programs in place focused on teaching children about racism, but I believe it's the adults who need anti-racist training. I'm not saying that kids can't be racist, but there tends to be a lack of expectation on teachers and other staff to address their own racism. In my experience, early childhood educators are some of the most politically conservative teachers. A child's experience in the classroom can shape them and set them on a path of success or failure; oppressive experiences from educators, therefore, must be addressed.

For example, there could be a situation in which working-class People of Color, who are possibly undocumented, cannot communicate in the same fashion as the teacher— regardless of whether that teacher is White or Black. Unfortunately, implicit biases due to racism, classism, and xenophobia can ultimately lead to a child in this situation being treated very poorly. I want to open a door to prevent this. I want all children to be able to trust their teachers.

*I'd also like to know about your cycling advocacy and activism related to public transportation. I know that has also been a part of your work for many years.*

First, let me explain that my family *loves* cars. My dad has always loved sports cars in particular. In 2006, I saw *An Inconvenient Truth* at the Santa Monica pier. At the time, I had a special mini blue-and-white convertible that I purchased after being on a waiting list for it. I *loved* that car. However, after watching the film, I sold my car within six months and thought that I would never drive again. I started a blog called the *Bus Bench* to document my experiences with public transportation. At one point, I moved to Boyle Heights while I was working in Compton. I started taking the bus back and forth between my home and work; it was horrible!

Being from LA, I knew poverty existed; but I never really understood poverty and racism in Los Angeles until I got on a bus. While on the Blue Line, I began to witness immense oppression. Ultimately, I started riding my bike after becoming so frustrated with the bus service on the east side of L.A. and South Central. I rode my bike from East L.A. to Compton, and I started writing about my experiences. I became the first editorial blog about transportation issues in Los Angeles. L.A. Metro had to start a blog because of me. I was so effective at making fun of them, including through the making of videos that demonstrated things like the difference in safety between the gold line in East L.A. and the gold line in Pasadena. I wrote about these issues on the blog from 2006 to 2012.

I love talking about history, bicycles, and safety. Currently, my work has gone beyond Los Angeles, and I'm now advocating for bicyclists on a national level. The most dangerous streets are in Black communities. The roads on which people are getting killed by cars are predominantly in neighborhoods of People of Color. I have been interested in these issues for a long time. When I got my master's from Pacific Oaks, my thesis was called *The Green Tricycle*. My theory was that, if every child, regardless of their ability to ride, could ride their green tricycle up the main street in their town, we'd have a perfect society. If we think about it, what would we need for a child to be able to survive on a green tricycle on a major street? You would need an infrastructure to support this, so that it would be perfectly normal and safe for the child. Everything would need to be connected to make it happen.

***Your transportation advocacy is related to your new initiative, Black Kids in Outer Space. Please tell me about this.***

Black Kids in Outer Space is a multimedia editorial news platform that uses videos, podcasts, photos, writing, and art to cover Africans and the African Diaspora in relation to space (transportation, environment, and urban planning policy). Our inspiration is the traditional Black media, and we strive to honor Ida B. Wells, Lucy Parsons, and the first Black-owned newspaper— the *Freedom Journal*, founded in 1827— in our coverage.

I created Black Kids in Outer Space to bring together my loves of art, Afrofuturism, Afrosurrealism, and urban planning. I want to talk about the Black community in transportation and urban planning in a way that is fun. I try to create narratives that bring joy to people and make Black people smile.

*I noticed while watching some of your video interviews for Black Kids in Outer Space that you often ask your guests, "What is your first memory of space?" I was intrigued by this. Why do you ask this question?*

I ask this question because I want to know what people see— in both the literal and figurative senses— when they look out into space. When I ask this question, some people bring up *Star Trek* or *Star Wars*. Some people bring up riding their bikes in the park, and others mention stars. Space can mean so many things for people. My first memory of space is riding my bicycle at Manhattan Beach with my mother.

*How do you continue to stay positive with your activism work?*

I stay positive by understanding that, while oppression is personal, I do not want to make what I do personal. I chip away at the system. I don't fight in my home, or in my social life. I work on the system at large, not on individuals. I connect with people and surround myself with people who support me.

## Ardeth De Vries

Old Dog Haven

www.OldDogHaven.org

—

"It's important that people know that they can make a difference."

*Ardeth De Vries has always loved dogs. After her retirement from a long career as an educator, she became involved with Old Dog Haven, a non-profit organization in western Washington that finds homes for abandoned, senior dogs. Currently, Old Dog Haven provides private homes for over 300 dogs. Ardeth is the author of the award-winning book* Old Dog Haven: Every Old Dog Has a Story to Tell *(Bennett & Hastings Publishing, 2014). She is currently the Executive Director of Old Dog Haven, has served as president of the Old Dog Haven Board of Directors, is the editor of the organization's blog and newsletter, and counsels others about end-of-life decisions for their dogs. Here, she discusses her work with Old Dog Haven; reflects on the many life lessons she has learned from dogs; and shares stories of some of the amazing dogs she has been honored to know.*

—

Considering who I am and what I'm all about as an adult, it might be reasonable to assume that, as a child, I spent my days rescuing stray dogs and hanging out with the family dog. Not so. Animals weren't welcome in our home because my father was afraid of dogs, so I had to be content with making friends with the neighborhood dogs. I remember going to New Jersey with my parents to visit my aunt— something I really didn't want to do; but my aunt had a dog named Lassie, so I was happy to make the trip because I *loved* being with Lassie. I was also very active in sports and interested in medicine. For as long as I can remember, I told adults who asked me what I was going to be when I grew up that I was going to be a doctor. (I'm not sure I've ever grown up, and I'm not a doctor.)

In college, I pursued the courses that you take for pre-med, but I didn't like any of them. The thought of taking more chemistry and biology instead of playing tennis or being around animals wasn't interesting to me. I just wanted to be a doctor without going to medical school. When I graduated from college, I had a double major in English and psychology and a minor in philosophy. I took hardly any science courses. That should tell you where my head was.

During my senior year, I was playing in a tennis match one day and, after the match, I returned to my dorm to find a notice on the bulletin board for a teaching job at a little high school in California. It was too late to apply for grad school, and I'd never been to California, so I figured I could be a teacher while I pursued graduate school. I ended up being a teacher for well over forty years— and yes, I did get my master's degree. I loved teaching and had a wonderful time with my students. For many years, I directed theater while I was teaching English, psychology, drama, and all kinds of other subjects. Later, I served as a high school counselor. When it came time for me to retire, Whidbey Island, Washington called to me, and I decided that this would be a wonderful place to live. (It is!)

I taught at the college here for a couple of years, until I learned about Old Dog Haven.

### How did you become involved with Old Dog Haven?

My involvement started in 2005. The organization was founded in 2004 by Judith and Lee Piper, when they decided they wanted to adopt a couple of older dogs from a local shelter in the Seattle area and, in doing so, realized that there was a tremendous need to provide homes for homeless senior dogs who found themselves in shelters.

I found out about Old Dog Haven when I was walking dogs at our local shelter. My dog-walking friend thought an organization that helped senior dogs was something I'd like to be a part of, and she was right; I contacted Judith, and the rest is history!

Once I became involved with Old Dog Haven, I jumped in with both feet, and it has consumed most of my time and energy for the past thirteen years or so. You could say my life has gone to the dogs— and I wouldn't have it any other way.

### What is it about dogs that makes you so committed to this work?

Maybe because of my teaching background, I view life as a visit filled with lessons that are there for us to learn if we choose to do so. Some of the most important lessons

I've ever learned in my life have come from dogs. One lesson is their ability to live in the present moment. People get involved with analyzing and thinking about tomorrow and focusing on the past; living in the moment and focusing on today is something that humans don't do very well. This is part of why I find dogs to be such great teachers. They know how to live in the moment.

Another lesson involves the human need to analyze and intellectualize in general, which is a flawed way to approach life. With dogs, you always know where you stand. It's a straight line of communication. Dogs process everything emotionally. It's all intuitive, and there's no second-guessing about what they feel or what they're thinking because they're so open. When your dog comes to you and puts his head on your knee, you know what he wants. No analysis necessary.

There is also the lesson of a lack of judgment. I've seen many, many dogs over the years who have come from horrible situations. Regardless of what went on in their past, we see dogs who are willing to trust a human again. They're willing to say, "Okay, I'm here now. Let's do this." Dogs are teachers, as far as I'm concerned. Human beings attempt to give unconditional love, but there are always strings and conditions. Dogs just do it.

Every one of us involved with Old Dog Haven shares the philosophy that senior dogs are to be valued, respected, and welcomed into the home as part of the family. Dogs shouldn't be tied up in the yard, kept in a crate, or end up in a shelter. What we see time and time again with senior dogs is that, at first, we may think the dog will not be around very long, but then, once they are given a second chance at happiness, they sometimes live for months and even *years* after. Others are only able to stay a short time because they're so hurt; but regardless of how long they live, they are all loved, valued, and respected.

### Do you have any stories to share about a special dog in your life?

I've loved all of the dogs who have lived with me, and many who haven't shared my home. One dog who comes to mind is Teddy. I refer to him as my touchstone. Teddy came to me when Judith, the Executive Director at the time, called one day and said, "This dog needs to be with you." He was found lying beside the dead body of the person with whom he'd lived his whole life. The man had been dead for four days, and Teddy was there by himself, holding a vigil. One of the neighbors realized that there hadn't been any activity in the house for days, so the police were called for a wellness check. That's how Teddy was found. I call him my touchstone because he had a way of teaching me— maybe more than any other dog I've known— about living in the moment.

Imagine what Teddy felt: alone for *four days* in the house with the dead body of his friend. I know he understood what happened, because dogs get death; they understand that it's just change. The loneliness he felt must have been palpable for him. Still, when he came to me, he marched right into the house like he *belonged* here. He knew where the water bowl was. He knew where the dog cookies were. He immediately went to the bed of the dog who had just left, which is why Judith had thought that perhaps I might have space for another dog. He knew he was home.

My partner of forty years had died not long before this, so I was going through a grieving process myself. Teddy was my live-in-the-moment dog. Those lessons came through him, loud and clear. He was a great guy. I learned a lot from him. I miss his physical presence, but what he taught me is still with me. I pass those lessons on whenever I can.

**I imagine this type of work may be sad at times. How do you stay positive and keep going?**

Staying positive is also something that dogs teach us. As an organization of individuals living with senior dogs, we understand that the dogs live in the moment, regardless of what happened in the past. On a related note, people often ask me, "How can you go to the animal shelter to walk dogs and see all of those dogs in cages?" My answer is always, "I figure that my time with them is my time to be with them in the moment." I focus on that– spending time with them and letting them know that they're important and helping them continue to be hopeful that their forever person will come to adopt them.

The same thing is true with the dogs at Old Dog Haven. What we are offering them is an opportunity to be happy dogs. In order to do that, we have to focus on them, rather than thinking about the people who abused, neglected, or abandoned them. You can't focus on the people because that kind of negative thinking contaminates what you're able to offer the dog. Being positive means looking for the good signs and improvements in their physical condition. It means cheering for the dog. Certainly, when it's time for them to leave, that sadness is there. That sense of loss is there; but I never think about it as being brokenhearted. I feel like my experiences with non-human animals have given me a heart that is able to feel things differently and to look at life in a little bit of a different way. My heart is never broken when a dog leaves; if anything, it's expanded.

What I've just said doesn't mean that we shouldn't grieve. Grieving is important because every dog deserves to be mourned and grieved. I once had a dog who was only with me for six hours, and it was immediately very clear that my role in his life was not to rehabilitate him but, instead, to release him from his body. He came with so many things wrong with him, and it was very obvious that he was in terrible pain and wouldn't be able to recover. My role in his life was to let him go— because nobody else would. He'd been in a boarding facility at which they simply ignored the issues he was having, and, as is often the case, his condition was misrepresented to Old Dog Haven.

What I have gained from the experiences of being with dogs— even the little guy who was only with me for six hours— is important. I'm so glad that he came to me, because he deserved to be remembered and honored. Grieving is an important thing; but, with every dog I have lived with, there's always been much more than a sense of loss. It's more of a sense of gain.

**What advice would you give someone who is interested in adopting a senior dog?**

One of the things we tell all of our foster families in Old Dog Haven is to let go of expectations. We don't know very much about the history of most of the dogs we take in; sometimes, we don't know anything at all. It's important to go easy with the dogs and let them show you what they need. Then, you can discover what the two of you can do together in terms of healing, having fun, and enjoying life.

The physical condition of the dog doesn't define who the dog is. I currently live with a dog named Corey. She ended up in a shelter, and no one claimed her. She was emaciated, anemic, covered with fleas, and she hadn't been spayed. The shelter did the best it could for her, and, as soon as the workers there spayed her, they realized she had cancerous mammary tumors. The tumors were removed, but the cancer had spread throughout her body. The shelter called Old Dog Haven and asked if we could provide a hospice situation for her. Corey came here.

Yes, it's true that there is cancer in Corey's body; but the cancer doesn't define who she is. She's a dog who's having an absolutely wonderful time. You should see her run on the beach! Every person she greets is her friend, and she's great with other dogs. Whatever went on in her past (she must have been used as a breeding machine), she's all done with that. She's perfectly content to be a happy dog. I have no idea how long she's going to be able to stay (she's already been here a year); but, to her, the fact that she has cancer isn't important. She's moving forward with her life, and I'm very happy to move with her.

There are dogs who come to us blind and/or deaf and have what we would perceive as a disability or a limitation. We might imagine that these perceived limitations would prevent them from fully being who they are, but they're not having any of it! One of my current dogs, Reggie, is both blind and deaf. He's 17– you should see him. There's nothing wrong with his radar, and there's nothing wrong with his nose. Sure, he's an old guy; but he still takes pleasure in a walk on the beach, a good meal, and a nice cuddle. He's being the best version of himself that he can be. It would be positive if humans could look at what's going on with them physically not as a limitation or a disability, but as simply being differently-abled.

### *Is there anything else you would like to share about rescue work with senior dogs?*

Something positive we are seeing now is that more and more people are willing to adopt a senior dog. It used to be, maybe twenty years ago, that if a dog was older than eight or nine, nobody would adopt the dog. People only went to shelters to adopt puppies and young dogs. More and more, I'm seeing that people are willing to take a chance on an older dog. Also, there are so many books being written about older dogs and senior dogs. There's awareness out there that an older dog has value. I love it. I'd like to see more people go to a shelter to adopt an older dog.

We need more rescue organizations like Old Dog Haven. We're only one of a couple in the United States that places dogs in private homes rather than shelters or sanctuaries. I would love to see more happening where people are willing to promote the value of senior dogs.

Through my work with Old Dog Haven, I'm constantly amazed and impressed with people. I know there's a lot going on in the world that speaks to a side of humanity that isn't positive; but, through Old Dog Haven, I see willingness in people to open their hearts and homes.

**_Do you see your work with senior dogs as something connected to other forms of justice work? If so, how does your work contribute to a better world for all beings?_**

Respecting and valuing all life forms creates a ripple effect that contributes to the reality of a peaceful world. Everything we do at Old Dog Haven is sent out into the universe and that positive energy serves to permeate the thinking and feeling of all beings. When people are positive about helping senior dogs, that energy serves to create a paradigm that will serve all interactions with people and animals. The world will be a better place if we allow ourselves to learn from animals and then pay it forward in any way we can. We are all one.

Making a difference means speaking and living your truth. If people walk their talk, then the path will become a road to a just and significant society.

# Sara Vander Zanden

Facing Homelessness

www.FacingHomelessness.org

—

"We believe that just being closer in proximity to marginalized communities helps to breakdown stereotypes."

*Several years ago, Sara Vander Zanden decided to follow her heart and pursue work she believes in; she is now the Executive Director for Facing Homelessness in Seattle, Washington. The nonprofit organization is built on inviting the Seattle community to be part of the solution to homelessness. According to Sara, "I believe that when we simply place compassion at the center of our lives, we can power a grassroots movement to end homelessness." Herein, she discusses her individual journey and several of the inspiring projects currently underway at Facing Homelessness.*

—

I was born in Grand Rapids, Michigan, and was raised in a small, agricultural community called Sparta. I was raised mostly by a single mom. She is the most resilient, strongest, and kindest person on the planet. My mom is still my best friend, and an absolute inspiration. I got so lucky! If she were to describe herself as a mother and me in my childhood, she would definitely say, "It takes a village." We were part of a really tight-knit community, in which I felt parented, loved, and cared for by pretty much every teacher and neighbor.

With my mom being on her own in such a small, conservative community, it felt like the whole community rallied around her to help care for me. Still, I can't tell you how desperate I was to leave Sparta, especially in my high school years. I was angsty and wanted to get out, travel, see the world, and just experience the depth and the breadth out there. I got my ticket out with a full-ride scholarship to the University of Michigan.

I will never forget opening my acceptance letter from the university. I instantly called my mom. I remember telling her, "Mom, I think I just got a scholarship to go to college. You have to come home and read it with me. I feel like I'm not reading it right." She drove home from work right away, and we stood there, looking over the letter. She called my Uncle Gary, saying, "Gary, you've got to come over and read this letter. I think Sara got a scholarship to college." My uncle came over and confirmed that I had a full ride to go to college. That whole night we sat on the kitchen floor crying and talking about everything that was possible. My mom didn't have a college education. It was never an opportunity she entertained. It was a big moment for me. We always knew I was going to go to college, but we didn't know how we were going to make it work financially, so receiving that letter was a major moment for us.

I was so excited to get out; then, of course, only after leaving and surviving in Ann Arbor, a bigger city, did I realize what a beautiful upbringing I had truly had. The community was very conservative, small, and sheltered; but it was also very loving. The people were hardworking and earnest. I have a deep appreciation for where I grew up, now.

*I can see the importance of community that continues to run through the work you do now. What did you study in college?*

I was in a program called organizational studies. It is an interdisciplinary program combining psychology, sociology, and economics. It is like a liberal arts approach to business. I was specifically interested in non-profit work, social movements, and social change. There was a lot of freedom in the program, so I directed my studies through a social lens.

*Tell me what happened after you graduated from college.*

In school, there was a lot of pressure. Many of my peers were going right out of school into consulting jobs for big firms, and they were making more money than I could ever imagine. At first, I thought, "Maybe I'm going to do that." After going to a couple of career fairs with those types of companies, I started getting this pit in my stomach. I had a college professor and mentor who said to me, "You know, there is a cost to applying to jobs like those. Would you actually turn down a $70,000-a-year offer?" I started crying because I believed I wouldn't be able to decline an offer for that much money, since I grew up in a family and community with limited resources. Despite knowing that a corporate future wouldn't fulfill me, I also knew that, once the money was on the table, I wouldn't be able to walk away from the stability and security it could offer.

Through that conversation and a couple of others, I determined that I was going to apply for more alternative positions, about which I was passionate. I knew it was a risk financially, but I just hoped that it would work. I ended up taking a job as a part-time seasonal farmer's market manager in Grand Rapids, Michigan. It was a unique program that was managed by the YMCA. The program was focused on connecting the many agricultural communities in West Michigan to the urban community, which had a lot of food deserts.

We had a "veggie van" that was a mobile farmer's market. We brought resources to schools, retirement communities, and low-income neighborhoods. We also had a corner store initiative that provided fresh food from my hometown to food deserts in urban neighborhoods. I worked on finding unique business opportunities and new markets for them. I was doing exactly what I wanted to be doing.

### How did you end up getting to Seattle and doing the work you do now with Facing Homelessness?

It was quite a journey from that first job out of college to now. I ended up leaving the non-profit sector to take a job at a communications firm in Grand Rapids. They did a good amount of philanthropic work. I did a lot of writing on the funding side, in project management, but for a private company. It was a big career shift. Shortly after that transition, my husband, Mike got a job offer in Seattle, and we moved across the country together.

For a short time, I worked for the same communications firm, but remotely, from Seattle. Through that experience, I realized how important it was for me to be working and living within my community.

Working remotely was not for me. I felt I really wasn't making an investment in my new city. Also, through living here, I started seeing right away the number of people living on the streets, sleeping in doorways and under bridges. A lot of people were moving to Seattle, especially a lot of millennials, for big tech jobs, and they weren't really becoming a part of the community.

I realized I was one of those people.

I started trying to build a network in the non-profit sector. I remember thinking I was open to any work related to social movements, but just *not* in the field of homelessness. I was very specific. It felt so overwhelming, and I honestly could not see where I would possibly be able to insert myself to have an impact for that community. I was meeting a lot of people, and I met with a woman who recommended Facing Homelessness. She said they were a grassroots organization, and they had an open position for an executive director. I met with the team at Facing Homelessness (Rex Hohlbein and Sarah Steilen) and pretty much instantly fell in love with the work.

I ended up getting two competing offers at the same time. The other one was technically a "better" offer; but, to my surprise and my husband's surprise, I picked the job with Facing Homelessness. I remember calling my husband, who was traveling for work at the time, and telling him, "I think I'm going to take this job in a field I know nothing about." He said, "I think you need to do it; and the moment you do this, Sara, we are declaring our little family's commitment to social justice. If you're ready to do that, let's do it." I haven't looked back.

*Tell me about the work Facing Homelessness does by starting with the organization's mission and one of its major initiatives: the BLOCK Project.*

Our mission at Facing Homelessness is to invite community to be a part of the solution to homelessness. This is tied to everything we do. We believe that just being closer in proximity to marginalized communities helps to breakdown stereotypes. The distance that society has created between different communities overcomplicates our relationships with others. When we simply cross the street and kneel down beside someone, all of the biased questions and preconceived notions we have about homeless people, such as "How did you get here? Are you 'lazy'? Are you into drugs?" begin to shift. All of those stereotypes fly away when we are sitting with someone. Our questions change to, "How are you? What's your name? How can I help?" Everything we do is to increase that proximity and reduce the distance that we have created between ourselves and the most vulnerable in our communities.

The BLOCK Project takes this to its pinnacle level by asking homeowners to host a block home in their backyard, which is a small, off-grid and fully self-sufficient home. Through this, we take the paradigm of, "Not in my backyard" and completely flip it on its head. We instead say, literally, "Yes, in my backyard!" Right now, a lot of people ask, "Why would I do that? Why would someone do that? Why would they open up their backyard?" We think that someday, it will be just as normal to think about your backyard as a platform for social justice as it is to think about your spare room as a potential income generator through AirBnB. Amazingly, in Seattle, we already have over one hundred homeowners who have come forward to say, "I want one in my backyard. How do I get on the list? Put one in my backyard next." We've seen a clear desire from the community to get involved. People are saying they do not want to be bystanders to the issue of homelessness. They don't want to see people suffering. We hear again and again that people don't know what to do. It's not that they don't want to help. They just don't know how to get started. The BLOCK Project provides people a really clear way to have an impact.

Facing Homelessness owns the BLOCK Project, but we always want to mention our most important partner, which is Block Architects. They're the architectural firm that helps us manage the construction side of the project. They work with contractors and do the architectural design.

### How far along are you with providing homes?

We currently have two homes. We are growing. Just like a non-profit start-up, everyday it's a new square peg in a new round hole. We're doing something that has never been done before, so everything— from the legal structure, to the financial structure, to the social services structure, to the architecture, to the office systems, and beyond— has to be created from scratch, on a scale commensurate with what we're trying to achieve.

It is really incredible! We have about seventy-five firms in the architecture, engineering, and construction industries who are engaged in this project and offering their services to us. We really couldn't do it without volunteer support.

Our first resident is Robert. It has been really amazing to see the experience this has been for Kim and Dan, his host family. They were committed to the opportunity of helping to change someone's life, but they did not expect their lives to change as well. They often share how their lives are enriched by just knowing their new neighbor. As someone who was experiencing homelessness, Robert had been kept outside of community and unable to participate in society.

**Another project that you work on is the Window of Kindness. What does that program focus on?**

The Window of Kindness is another one of our programs that, like the BLOCK Project, is about creating proximity. It's kind of a beginning step, I suppose, if you think about our programs on a spectrum. People living outside come to our window at the Facing Homelessness offices to get items, such as tents, tarps, sleeping bags, backpacks, socks, and other essentials for staying warm and dry. Volunteers come to our window and help to distribute those materials. Most importantly, they provide an opportunity for connection. We say all of the time, "The most important thing that we offer out of our window is connection." We have people come to the window frequently. The window is a kind of symbol for the connections that we want to be taking place in our community.

*I understand photojournalism is also part of Facing Homelessness. This is evidenced on the website and through all of the stunning photographs!*

Yes, that is how our work actually began. Our founder, Rex Hohlbein, who has been an architect for thirty years, started meeting people who were sleeping on the streets, and realized that they were not matching up to the negative stereotypes that are so pervasive around homelessness. He wanted to share their photos and stories with the people he knew, so he started a Facebook page. He didn't really know if it would go anywhere. The community, however, responded to what he was doing, and they shared their desire to be a part of the solution. The initiative ended up becoming the non-profit, Facing Homelessness.

Rex's architectural firm became a drop-in and drop-off center for community members following the Facebook page, eager to help someone in need. He wasn't getting any architectural work done, so he closed his practice and started Facing Homelessness. A really amazing statistic about our Facebook page is that we now have around 50,000 followers and, so far, every single time we shared someone's story and made a request on their behalf, the community has met the need. This has included a pair of boots, getting a car out of impound, and even paying two months' rent— which is a lot of money in Seattle. The community's response was what gave us the initial confidence to start the BLOCK Project, and it continues to keep us going.

*How do you believe your work contributes to making the world better for marginalized people?*

Every day, forty-one people move to Seattle and only fourteen units of housing are built. Homelessness and wealth disparity are growing at unprecedented rates. Existing models for providing housing and human services are not equipped to meet the growing demand. This impacts all of us; none of us can truly thrive when so many of our neighbors are suffering.

We hope to create change by leveraging community, which is responsive, nimble, and eager to get involved; so, we empower communities to be a part of the solution.

## Janet Holmes

Animal Rescue Photographer

www.FrogOutOfWater.ca

"I committed to become vegan just after my fiftieth birthday."

—

*Janet Holmes uses her artistic talent in photography as a form of animal rights activism. Janet came to photography, veganism, and activism later in life, around age fifty; and, although she continues to work in her "day job" as a lawyer, she devotes much of her free time to photographing nonhuman animals— especially rescued farm animals. Her self-published book* Why Would Anyone Rescue a Chicken? *documents one of her recent projects photographing rescued chickens in their homes with their human family members. In just a few short years, Janet has received many awards for her photography, including the People's Choice Award for The Fence: 2018 (North America's Largest Traveling Photography Exhibition). She has also participated in solo and group exhibitions and numerous juried exhibitions. Herein, Janet discusses her awakening to animal rights and how she uses photography to bring awareness of nonhuman animal rights to others. Her story demonstrates how it is never too late to begin an activist life and start making profound contributions toward a better world.*

—

I was born in Sault Ste. Marie, Ontario, on Lake Superior; but I grew up on the coast of British Columbia with my mother, my father, his mother, and my sister. Before they retired, my father worked as an engineer and my mother worked as a nurse.

I spent most of my childhood and adult life immersed in a world of words. Partly that was due to aptitude and interest. I loved reading and writing from a very early age, and my favorite place (until quite recently) was the library. I also think my interest in books flowed from some difficulties I had with my vision, including very limited depth perception. I found it somewhat difficult to navigate the world and engage with people I had a hard time recognizing; so, I turned inward, to the printed page.

I would put my books aside to spend time with other animals, though. We shared our home with various non-human companions over the years, including some rescued animals. I was also that kid who could be found talking to frogs and crawling under the pick-up truck to say hello to the garter snake.

From an early age, I had in mind that I might become a lawyer. There were lawyers and judges in my family. I was always the kid in class who was willing to speak up and question how the adults were interpreting the rules. In high school, I conducted an undercover investigation into discriminatory hiring practices at a local employer that hired lots of students, and then successfully brought a complaint before the BC Human Rights Tribunal for gender discrimination.

After high school, I studied history and English at the University of Victoria on Vancouver Island and then the University of British Columbia in Vancouver. I was then accepted into the University of Toronto Law School and completed a general law degree there, followed by a Master of Securities Law at Osgoode Hall Law School (also in Toronto).

### What happened once you got to law school?

I loved it! I found it really interesting. I had amazing classmates and teachers. It was a good fit. At the time, there were no specialized courses in animal law, as there are today. I don't know what would have happened with my path if there was an animal law course back then. My life might have ended up very different.

I was interested mainly in business law, probably because the opportunities for stable employment at high salaries were greater in business law than in fields like criminal law or social justice. I had seen my friends' parents get laid off in high school, I'd had trouble finding summer jobs at the university, and I graduated from law school during the post-Black Friday downturn in the economy. I think one of the things that had been motivating me was the feeling that I needed to be able to have a career that would allow me to take care of myself. I wasn't going to rely on anybody else.

I've had a very interesting legal career at law firms in Toronto and New York, at government agencies, for an international organization in Paris, and in-house at a corporation. I continue to work as a lawyer today, specializing in knowledge management and communications.

### During your early college years and later, in law school, did you still have an interest in animals?

I was always interested in animals and enjoyed spending time with them, but I didn't construct my life around them. I was just focused on getting through school, and then coping with the long work hours that junior lawyers are expected to deliver. After I had been working for a few years, I adopted a cat, who I named Emma, because I saw a sign on the bathroom wall at my law firm that said, "Somebody needs to adopt this cat, or she's going to a shelter." Emma turned my apartment into a home, and we spent the next eighteen years together, until she passed away in 2012.

**Can you tell me about how your work with nonhuman animals came to be?**

It started around 2013. I had been working in a very demanding role in New York during the financial crisis, and, as the crisis started to recede a little, I began to feel that it was important to do more in the community, as well as carve out time for myself. Throughout my career, I had often volunteered as a coach, teacher, and mentor for teens and young adults. I found that work fulfilling, but not captivating.

Then, all of a sudden, two experiences came together. My husband and I were planning a trip to Borneo (mainly to experience the wild animals there), and we decided to give each other good cameras and learn how to use them. We enrolled in a photography course shortly thereafter. At the time, I had also started to think about volunteering with an animal rescue group. I had stayed away from this type of work my whole adult life, and I think it was because I believed that I couldn't handle the heartbreak. By 2013, however, I realized that nonhuman animals needed me more than I needed to be comfortable. I started to search for an opportunity to volunteer with a rescue group.

Meanwhile, we had kittens at home, so, naturally, I photographed them for my course homework. I began getting feedback from instructors and others that my photography showed some promise. Some of my teachers suggested that my visual impairments, especially my poor depth perception and inability to see sharply, helped me develop my composition skills as a photographer fairly quickly. I see the way a camera does, in two dimensions, and I focus (out of necessity) on shapes and strong lines in photographs.

In the Fall of 2013, I started volunteering with Mighty Mutts / Ollie's Place, photographing dogs and cats to facilitate their adoption. At about the same time, I started volunteering with the Wild Bird Fund in New York City, which rescues and rehabilitates wild animals. It also takes care of chickens and ducks who escape from live markets or are dumped by humans to fend for themselves.

**Did your experiences as a photographer with the rescue group and as a caregiver with the Wild Bird Fund lead you to become vegan?**

Yes, that happened maybe about six months into these new experiences. As I spent more time with them, holding them in my hands as a caregiver and looking at them through the lens of my camera, I became uncomfortable with the reality that I was caring for *these* animals, but eating others. I did the kind of research a lot of people do when they start to feel like that. I became aware of the way nonhuman animals are treated in our food system, and I became increasingly uncomfortable. I started to look for the "humane" alternatives and realized there was no such thing. Even what was marketed as "humane" involved cruelty and, of course, the animals were still killed, regardless.

There was a turning point for me in the Spring of 2014. I was following the story of wild turkeys on Staten Island, NY, who were being threatened with extermination. Some groups got together to protest, and several sanctuaries— including Catskill Animal Sanctuary, north of New York City— volunteered to provide homes for the turkeys. I discovered that it was possible to tour the sanctuary and see the rescued animals (including the turkeys) there. Even better, I learned that CAS had a guesthouse (called the "Homestead"), where you could stay overnight. I said to my husband, "Let's celebrate our wedding anniversary and my fiftieth birthday at Catskill Animal Sanctuary."

When you book a stay at the Homestead, they send you a note beforehand that asks you to respect their vegan principles and not bring any animal products into the Homestead. I read that note and thought, "Of course, I won't bring any food derived from animals." Literally about thirty minutes before we drove up to the Sanctuary, I looked at the note again and realized they didn't mean only food. My husband and I started stripping off all of our clothes made with animal products, emptying our suitcases of personal care products made from animals, and we even had to leave a suitcase with leather handles behind. That was a real catalyst for me. I realized how embedded all of these animal products were in our everyday lives. It was shocking.

The next morning, we woke up and walked down to the sanctuary to meet the resident animals. It was extraordinarily joyful and peaceful. My most memorable encounter was with a turkey named Daisy. She was a white turkey that is sometimes called a broiler. These turkeys are bred to grow large very quickly, so that they can be slaughtered when they are only a couple of months old. Luckily, she was rescued at a young age and brought to Catskill Animal Sanctuary. Because of how she had been bred, she had grown very large and had some difficulty walking. But she still enjoyed life. I can still remember how wonderful it was to hear her and the other turkeys chatter.

In one of the photographs I took of Daisy, she was standing under a sign that had the quote: "Be the change you wish to see in the world."

I looked at that photograph when I got back to my room and said to myself, "Yes, I will." I committed at that moment to becoming vegan. I have to be honest and say it took me a little while to transition, because I'm a picky eater when it comes to vegetables; but I soon figured out how to make and eat tasty, nutritious broccoli-free meals.

*That is a beautiful story. I love how it was an epiphany of one moment and you took the necessary steps to change your life. It is inspiring that it occurred later in your life, and you did not hesitate to move forward with what felt right.*

Yes, I committed to become vegan just after my fiftieth birthday. I stopped eating land animals immediately and then transitioned to the point where I would sometimes eat dairy, eggs, or fish when I was away from home. Then, I gave away all of my clothes and other products that were made from animals. Over the course of about a year and a half, I became fully vegan.

**The other aspect of your story I find inspiring is how you became a photographer and activist later in life.**

Definitely. In some ways, I have lived a very conventional life. I still have my conventional career and day job, but photography has become an extremely important part of my life. I think there are ways to create space for what is important in your life.

**What would you tell somebody reading this interview, perhaps an older person, who is interested in becoming vegan or becoming an activist in some way, but they are not sure how to begin?**

I think I would encourage them to pay close attention to their feelings about what drives them and what motivates them the most. Some people might choose to pursue activities that are similar in type to what they've done before; for example, a lawyer might donate her services to an activist group that needs her help. Or, like me, you might be motivated to do something completely different from your prior experience. You might have to push yourself out of your comfort zone, but, if you care deeply about the cause, you can find the willpower.

*When people see your photographs on a gallery wall, your website, or another space, what are you hoping they take away?*

Overall, I hope they will look at the nonhuman animal in the image and see an individual. They will see a "he" or a "she" or a "they" and not an "it." I hope they will realize that the animal is not that different from their pet at home and that the animal's differences does not take away from their personhood or justify their ill treatment. I hope that if they start to have that recognition that they might start to question their relationship to the nonhumans that we exploit.

*Please tell me about your book* **Why Would Anyone Rescue a Chicken?**

That project started in January 2017. It was shortly before the inauguration of Donald Trump, and there were news stories about potential cuts to reproductive health care and the possibility of Roe v. Wade being overturned. At that time, I met a hen at the Wild Bird Fund who was suffering from severe, chronic reproductive illness including a prolapsed uterus. Her ailments are common for laying hens due to selective breeding over decades in which they have been physiologically manipulated to produce hundreds of eggs a year. Their bodies can't handle it. Her veterinary bills were getting costly. Someone mentioned there were people who adopted chickens in situations like hers, so I set out trying to find a home for her. I discovered a network of vegans, primarily women, who rescue chickens and live with them.

I thought about how many women and other people with vaginas still struggle to obtain adequate, affordable reproductive health care— and how, in turn, we are socialized to exploit hens' reproductive systems. It seems that, even across species, society expects to dictate how these beings use their bodies. I decided to make portraits of the chickens and their rescuers to pay tribute both to the birds who have suffered so much and the people who have spent so much time, money and love caring for them. To date, I've photographed about twenty-five families in the mainland United States, Puerto Rico, Canada, the United Kingdom, and Norway. Along with the photographs, I included information about the health issues chickens face in the egg-laying industry. I donate half of my profits to individual rescuers or to the Microsanctuary Resource Center, which provides grants to people to pay for reproductive healthcare services for chickens.

I'm continuing with this project. Through it, I've come to understand a little better how pervasive and damaging the dominant views of gender and reproductive function can be. We have been socialized to assign monetary value to the bodies of hens, and so we breed, restrain, and exploit them until they die. Roosters are considered worthless and often thrown out like trash. This project began with a focus on women and hens because I saw a parallel in society's treatment of them, but now it needs to break away from the system it sought to criticize, which values, or devalues, people for their reproductive function.

It's also a priority for me right now to be more representative and inclusive in terms of culture, ethnicity, and gender in these portraits since many of the vegans portrayed in the media are white and cisgender. I hope that

People of Color, trans people, and non-binary people—vegan or not— will see my portraits and be able to see themselves represented and included in the movement. I also hope they can picture themselves in a home, full of love and peace, that they share with a farmed animal companion, like a chicken.

***When you think of your photography as a form of activism for the animals, do you see your work as contributing to a better world for all beings?***

I hope so. I think it is important to do what we can to reach people in different ways. When it comes to injustices people respond to different things: imagery, sound, words, and other means. The imagery I showcase in my photography has different purposes. One is definitely activism. My photographs are able to get human people to reconsider their relationship to nonhuman animals. I also think that showing portraits of rescued farm animals, who are safe and loved, can be a source of validation for people who are already involved in animal rights work. And I also hope that my portraits of animals preserve a positive memory for their caregivers since many of these rescued animals do not live long lives. I want my photographs to be a gift and a positive reminder of what can be accomplished when we choose to re-examine our role in this world and how that affects others.

STACY RUSSO

# Edwin Ramirez

Comedian / Poet

www.RollingEddie.com

—

"The stories I share have always had an intention behind them of letting others know about everyday ableism."

*Edwin Ramirez uses stand-up comedy as a form of activism to build connections and make his audiences aware of everyday ableism and racism. Edwin was born with cerebral palsy and uses a wheelchair for mobility. Comedy has become not only a vehicle for Edwin to awaken others to the ableism he encounters on a daily basis, but also a form of self-therapy. In addition to his work as a comedian, Edwin is a poet. His poetry will be featured in a forthcoming book on racial profiling in Switzerland. Herein, he shares his early life experiences growing up with cerebral palsy and how he now uses personal stories in his comedic performances to awaken others and, ultimately, create a more just and compassionate world.*

—

I was born in Zurich, Switzerland, in 1990. Zurich is where my parents met. My father is Dominican, and he's first generation in Switzerland. My mother is Spanish, and she's second generation. They went on vacation, and they came back married. They ended up not getting along, so my father left us. Then they had a fling a year later, and that's how my younger brother came to be. My parents separated again and tried to live together once more, for a few weeks, when I was about nine years old. They were constantly fighting, so it didn't work out.

Even though I've always wanted my father more in my life, I understand that maybe it is better this way. I was pretty much raised by my mom and the Spanish side of my family. My mom holds a lot of grudges against my dad's family, so she tried to build walls against them. This also reflects how we live now.

My brother is lighter-skinned than I am. When he tells people that he's Spanish, they don't give it a second thought. Meanwhile, for me, my Dominican side is not something I can hide even if I wanted to do so. It's unfair, but it's impacted how we live. I didn't experience a lot of racism until I started to grow out my hair. There was always some kind of deniability, but now there isn't.

I was born with my disability, which is due to having been born three months early. My brain had a lack of oxygen, which is why some of my brain cells died. This caused me to have cerebral palsy. Fortunately, in my case, it only affects my legs, without affecting my mind; and it doesn't worsen over time. I can basically live with it the way I'm living now. I can plan my life around it. My disability was always very visible to me. I was aware of how different it made me and my family. My family members tried to deal with it as positively as they could. They always wanted me to learn how to walk when I was younger.

The more I learned how my body worked, the more I learned that I would never be able to walk. I also learned that it wouldn't be a problem for me, as long as I have a good wheelchair and an accessible house. I had to teach my family to be okay with the fact that I'm never going to walk. I was about sixteen when it hit them; I was already accepting it. Understanding my reality is why I had to mature earlier than I normally would have.

### Have you always lived in Switzerland?

Yes. I've been living my whole life in Switzerland. I went to a school specifically for people with disabilities. We didn't have grades, so it was really hard to measure the students' progress individually. We also had a lot of physical therapy during the week, in the same building. I have always found it difficult to tell or compare myself and my academic progress to people who didn't have a disability. It felt very segregated, and, for the longest time after, I've had feelings that I have to catch up to other people. I only went into a regular school when I started my apprenticeship for office work and accounting, around age seventeen.

I've always felt like I had lost so much time; but, over the years, I've realized I've turned out a lot smarter than I thought. This has helped me to relax. Also, being on stage as a comedian helped me realize that while my disability makes my life quite different, it's still very relatable to people.

### Let's talk about your work as a comedian. How did you start?

I face a lot of everyday ableism and racism. Most ableism comes from people not knowing how to deal with it. They usually ask a lot of ignorant questions. Humor is a very good way to break the ice, dispel their fears, and have them treat me as they would other people. I started using humor as a defense mechanism, or as a way of getting by.

It was about 2015 when a group of my friends asked me if I wanted to tell my stories on stage. They told me they found the things I was saying to be quite funny. I tried, and I was immediately hooked. I haven't stopped since, because it is so fun! It's also a form of therapy. Although I am using humor, I am also mindful of making sure that people realize that these are real things happening to me, and I'm not making light of it. There's a balancing act in which I want people to laugh, but I don't want to make it too ridiculous. There is still a frustration behind my situation.

**What was it like that first time you got on stage, in 2015?**

I wasn't able to eat all day because I was so nervous! I remember it was an open mic for comedians, musicians, and poets. Before my turn, a professional comedian showed up incognito to test out his new material. Not only was I anxious for my first time up on stage, but also because there was a professional comedian before me who did a really good set.

In the end, my set turned out amazing. The people loved it. I loved it. I went right back up the next month, when they had the event again.

*What would you tell someone reading this who may want to do something like comedy or some other form of public performance, but who is afraid?*

I think what's really important is to find a venue where you feel safe and where you know that you have a welcoming audience. It can be really reassuring to have people there who you know, so bring some friends along! Just try it a few times. I know now, looking back, some of the jokes I told back then, I'd still tell them. Now, I tell them very differently, because I've had much more experience telling stories in public. It's a process. It's fun! That's also a very important part of it. Just have fun with it, and don't worry too much.

*Did you feel from the beginning that what you were doing with your comedy was some form of activism or social justice work?*

Not exactly. The stories I share have always had an intention behind them of letting others know about everyday ableism. I wanted to let people know that it happens. I started thinking more about activism after my second time on stage. A comedy scout who was in the audience asked if I wanted to do a newcomer set for a show that was going to be aired on television. I said, "Oh my God, yes!" As I prepared, I became very aware that I can reach a lot of people by doing these shows. It made me more aware about what I talk about and how I'm going to use this time on stage. So, it morphed into becoming a form of activism very quickly.

*When you are performing, do you also talk about your experiences with racism?*

Yes, I talk about the racism that I experience in my daily life. I also have bits about my Dominican or Spanish history that I bring into it. It is a challenge. I need to figure out how to take a topic that's not funny, such as racial profiling, and turn it into a story that's humorous, but also poignant. The story can't lose its edge and importance. Right now, I'm also trying to figure out how to talk about topics that interest me that have nothing to do with my personal life, because I want to be able to branch out a bit.

**I have never been to where you live in Switzerland, but I understand it is very white.**

Absolutely. I just went to New York for the first time last year, in October, and it was amazing to see so many People of Color! Coming back, I realized, once again, just how white Switzerland is. It's wild! I constantly feel exotic here, and, even though I live in the part of the city that has a lot of immigrants, it's still just a small part of the city. Switzerland is very big on assimilation, and that is part of its racism. Even People of Color who grew up here don't usually talk about race. They reject where they are from and their identity as immigrants. People need to know it's okay to be proud of where you're from, and it doesn't have to be a bad thing. There's this false dichotomy that you're either an immigrant or Swiss when, in reality, both of these things can be true at the same time.

There's also this idea that Switzerland is very neutral and peaceful and welcoming, but that's just on the surface. Once you've lived here for a while, you realize there are a lot of microaggressions related to racism. Once you start challenging this country, people start becoming very defensive and sometimes even aggressive.

## When you are performing, is the audience mostly white?

Yes— almost entirely. When I'm in Zurich, it's a bit more mixed; but it's always majority white. When I'm in the countryside, then it's even worse. There will be a sea of all-white faces, which makes it really difficult for some stories to connect with people. If you talk about race or racism, white people will become defensive and pride themselves on their color blindness. I have to be mindful and prepared to experience a *lot* of push back.

I'm hopeful that using my autobiographical style helps people put themselves in my shoes for the time I'm on stage. I'm not entirely sure how much they really get it or don't, but there have been some positive times. The other day, I met a person who saw me on television. They approached me and said they now know to not touch Black people's hair. This was something they didn't think about before; it was heart-warming to see the impact I had made.

I also remember this time when an elderly man came up to me and told me that he has a disabled son. He said a lot of the stories that I told on stage reminded him of occurrences he had when he was with his son. He was glad that somebody was talking about it on stage and that it was being acknowledged in that way. As long as I can feel that it's making a difference, I will keep doing it.

*It's beautiful to hear the impact on those people, because I believe it does not stop there. It spreads with even one person sharing your impact with others.*

*Let's move into another aspect of your life. I understand you are a poet.*

Poetry is something I do very sporadically, and mostly for myself. I started writing poetry when I was about fourteen. I write when I get a strong feeling that I need to express myself. Even if what I write doesn't make much sense at first, that is okay, because it's poetry. I can take that feeling and see where it leads me. I'm very happy that one of my poems is going to be published in a book collecting studies and poetry on racial profiling in Switzerland.

*That's wonderful! So, it sounds like poetry has been part of your life before comedy. Would you say poetry has been a form of therapy or self-care?*

Absolutely, absolutely! What I find really interesting about poetry is that when you start a poem, you start out with one emotion; then, over the course of the poem, that emotion transforms into a different one. That's probably my favorite part of writing poetry, because you can feel as if it's actually happening *inside of you*. You are acknowledging something that you were feeling, and you are working through it with your mind. For me, that's the beauty of poetry: being in conversation with yourself and finding healing through that.

I've only read my poetry to a live audience once. It was for a small exhibition for a local artist of color. He asked various other artists of color to perform. I realized performing a poem out loud is quite different from just reading it to yourself. When I read it out loud, it didn't sound how it had sounded in my head, so I discovered I may need to make some adjustments, depending on the delivery of the poem. It's an interesting process.

***Considering all of the forms of discrimination and racism you have experienced, how do you stay positive with your comedy and everything else in your life?***

A lot of more privileged artists don't want to upset the status quo, which has been incredibly frustrating for me over time. What helps me is when I can talk to other artists whose work is consciously political– artists who entertain, but also want to change the world. It also helps to be around and talk to friends who have experiences like I do. Sometimes it can also just be partying among Queer people or People of Color and enjoying life together. That can be healing.

There are definitely times, though, when it does get to be too much, and I'm completely drained. I may have a performance in which people didn't really get it. Maybe the audience had fun, but it was clear that it didn't see my performance as anything more than entertainment. That can be incredibly frustrating.

One time, there was a jury at a performance. It was for a well-known contest in Switzerland. After the first round, I received feedback from the jury that my material was too heavy, and they couldn't bear to listen for longer than ten minutes. I was devastated because these stories are based on my actual life. I am already presenting a sanitized version of my daily reality, but the jurors were so sheltered that they couldn't even deal with *that!* It's important to acknowledge when there is anger, frustration, and pain, because it can also become the basis for new material!

**When someone sees you in your wheelchair and they may have stereotypes and biases, what would you want to tell them?**

I would like to say that, depending on the situation, they are free to ask me questions if they frame their questions in a respectful manner. I might not want to talk about something at any given time, so I would like people to be aware of that; but, otherwise, I'm happy to answer questions and talk about my life. Stories connect us and help us understand other people. They are a way to understand the differences among us and figure out how to level the playing field. Hopefully, through these stories and connections, we can start building a better world.

# 3 QUESTIONS:

# DISCUSSION AND SELF-REFLECTION

1. Was there an interview to which you felt especially connected? Why do you believe you felt this connection?

2. Do you feel inspired by a specific form of activism? If so, why?

3. After having read through the different types of activism that everyday people have done in their communities, their humble beginnings, and their inspirations, what does it mean to you to be an activist?

4. In reading from a wide variety of communities, have you become more willing to learn more about and address stereotypes and misconceptions that add to forms of oppression, such as rac-

ism, transphobia, classism, homelessness, xenophobia, body shaming, and speciesism?

5. Sonya Renee Taylor and Hilary Kinavey perform
work related to body positivity. Have you experienced body image issues, or what Taylor labeled
as "body terrorism?" If so, will you make a commitment to yourself to work towards embracing
yourself and your body?

6. Carol J. Adams discusses the daily practice of
keeping a journal, and Marisela Gomez discusses
the positive impact of mindfulness. Do you have
a similar practice to help you stay focused and
guide your own social justice practice? If not, can
you think of a way that such a practice could be
helpful in your own life and activism?

7. Michelle Carrera discusses involving her young
son in her activist work. If you have children in
your life, how can you involve them in working
towards a better world?

8. Both Kamekə Brown and Ardeth DeVries discuss
the lifechanging impact of working with non-
human animals and opening their homes to
adopted dogs. What do you think is the importance of interspecies connections and activism?

9. If you currently consume or use animals in any
form, did reading the interviews of activists who
are vegan make you question whether your activism should include non-human animal advocacy?

10. Sonya Renee Taylor shares the inspiring story of changing her life spontaneously and pursuing a dream of being a poet. Is there something you would like to do for a better world that would require a significant change? What steps could you put in place to realize this dream?

11. Edwin Ramirez discusses the way in which they are able to highlight their real-life experiences with ableism through comedy. If you are an able-bodied person, how can you work towards making your community accessible for those that are affected by systemic ableism?

12. Aquila Hope and Bamby Salcedo discuss the experiences of Trans People of Color in the U.K. and U.S. While their experiences may be difficult to understand for people born their assigned gender at birth, their stories remind us that our experiences and understanding of the world is uniquely ours. Can you make a commitment to respecting and standing up for the rights of people even if their experiences are vastly different to your own?

13. Several of the interviews examine the relationship between art, art-making, creativity, and activism. How do you think the arts have had an important role in social justice?

14. Looking at the issues facing your community, do you feel you can make the commitment to support a project or organization in your area, or start

your own form of activism?

15. What does it mean to have privilege over other communities? How can you use your privilege to raise the voices of those that have less privileges?

# 4 WITH GRATITUDE

I am thankful for my brother, David, and the amazing force of support he has been in my life as a writer. He was such an awesome big brother: buying multiple copies of my books to give to friends and finding a way, during his busy life, to set alarms so he would not miss any of my live radio interviews. I can still hear how he used to tell me, "You're golden!" when I doubted myself. My brother also provided me with immeasurable support when helping me overcome domestic abuse. While I was working on this project, he lost his voice and mobility due to the horrible condition known as ALS, or Lou Gehrig's Disease. My brother passed away on January 22, 2019. I am thankful for his wife, Linda, who cared for him with such compassion during this difficult time.

I am also thankful for my partner, Steven Soto, who has provided amazing support and endured many anxiety-filled moments related to my writing and difficult personal matters during this project. You, Steven, are a beautiful and magical soul. Thank you, Joni. I am thankful for Elise Bernal, Hillary Fielding, Mario Arreola, Ruth King, Julie Artman, Annie Knight, Irene Felipe, Nina Clements, Stephanie Keefer, and Laura Beth Bachman. Thank you, Victoria Schlicht. To everyone who agreed to participate in this amazing project– thank you so very much. I am grateful for your time. Finally, I have much gratitude for Julia Feliz Brueck and her wonderful Sanctuary Publishers. While working on this project, I came across the book *Veganism in an Oppressive World: A Vegans of Color Community Project,* published by Sanctuary Publishers. I read the book and immediately reached out to Julia to see if she would be willing to be interviewed. Many months after the interview, Julia saw that I was looking for a publisher. She agreed to read my proposal, and here we are! Julia was much more than a publisher; she was a collaborator. Her support, recommendations, and detailed interaction with the manuscript made the book better. I can't think of a more ideal publisher for this book. Thank you, Julia!

# 5 ABOUT STACY RUSSO

Stacy Russo, a community college librarian and professor at Santa Ana College, is a writer, poet, and artist. She believes in lifelong learning and the power of personal story. Stacy credits the punk rock movement of her teenage years with her political awakening and journey to veganism. Her books include *Love Activism* (Litwin Books); *We Were Going to Change the World: Interviews with Women from the 1970s/1980s Southern California Punk Rock Scene* (Santa Monica Press); *Life as Activism: June Jordan's Writings from The Progressive* (Litwin Books); and *The Library as Place in California* (McFarland). Her articles, poetry, and reviews have appeared in *Feminist Teacher, Feminist Collections, American Libraries, Counterpoise, Library Journal, Chaffey Review, Serials Review,* and the anthology *Open Doors: An Invitation to Poetry* (Chaparral Canyon Press). She holds degrees from the University of California, Berkeley; Chapman University; and San Jose State University.

STACY RUSSO